HAPPY BIRTHD

TO BESTEST WIFE

SATURDAY

26TH FEB 2005.

FROM YOUR LOVING HUSBAND

X   Michael   X

FRANCIS FRITH'S

HERTFORDSHIRE

LIVING MEMORIES

TOM DOIG is a social historian researching rural life in the 19th and 20th century. He is well known for his books on local history and for his radio and television programmes. During the 1980's, he held the post of Director of the Cambridge and County Folk Museum. Tom is currently running a number of lecture series for the Workers Education Association based in Cambridge as well as giving talks to local history, amenity and family history groups. He lives in a remote rural part of north Hertfordshire in a converted cattle shed built during the 1840's as part of a model farmstead. A qualified teacher and automobile engineer, he is interested in promoting history and engineering in his local primary school where he oversees a weekly engineers club. When relaxing from his history research, Tom devotes his time to the restoration of a vintage-style sports car and helping to run a Cambridgeshire motor racing team.

FRANCIS FRITH'S
PHOTOGRAPHIC MEMORIES

HERTFORDSHIRE
LIVING MEMORIES

TOM DOIG

First published in the United Kingdom in 2004 by
Frith Book Company Ltd

Hardback Edition 2004
ISBN 1-85937-524-3

British Library Cataloguing in Publication Data

Francis Frith's Hertfordshire Living Memories
Tom Doig

Frith Book Company Ltd
Frith's Barn, Teffont,
Salisbury, Wiltshire SP3 5QP
Tel: +44 (0) 1722 716 376
Email: info@francisfrith.co.uk
www.francisfrith.co.uk

Printed and bound in Great Britain

Front Cover: **RICKMANSWORTH,** *Church Street 1952*
R33027t
Frontispiece: **HEMEL HEMPSTEAD,** *Rock and
Roll Statue and Water Garden c1960* H255041

*The colour-tinting is for illustrative purposes only, and is not intended to be
historically accurate*

CONTENTS

FRANCIS FRITH
VICTORIAN PIONEER

FRANCIS FRITH, founder of the world-famous photo-graphic archive, was a complex and multi-talented man. A devout Quaker and a highly successful Victorian businessman, he was philosophical by nature and pioneering in outlook.

By 1855 he had already established a wholesale grocery business in Liverpool, and sold it for the astonishing sum of £200,000, which is the equiva-lent today of over £15,000,000. Now a very rich man, he was able to indulge his passion for travel. As a child he had pored over travel books written by early explorers, and his fancy and imagination had been stirred by family holidays to the sublime mountain regions of Wales and Scotland. 'What lands of spirit-stirring and enriching scenes and places!' he had written. He was to return to these scenes of grandeur in later years to 'recapture the thousands of vivid and tender memories', but with a different purpose. Now in his thirties, and captivated by the new sci-ence of photography, Frith set out on a series of pio-neering journeys up the Nile and to the Near East that occupied him from 1856 unti 1860.

INTRIGUE AND EXPLORATION

These far-flung journeys were packed with intrigue and adventure. In his life story, written when he was sixty-three, Frith tells of being held captive by ban-dits, and of fighting 'an awful midnight battle to the very point of surrender with a deadly pack of hungry, wild dogs'. Wearing flowing Arab costume, Frith arrived at Akaba by camel sixty years before Lawrence of Arabia, where he encountered 'desert princes and rival sheikhs, blazing with jewel-hilted swords'.

He was the first photographer to venture beyond the sixth cataract of the Nile. Africa was still the mys-terious 'Dark Continent', and Stanley and Livingstone's historic meeting was a decade into the future. The conditions for picture taking confound belief. He laboured for hours in his wicker dark-room in the sweltering heat of the desert, while the volatile chemicals fizzed dangerously in their trays. Back in London he exhibited his photographs and was 'rap-turously cheered' by members of the Royal Society. His reputation as a photographer was made overnight.

VENTURE OF A LIFE-TIME

Characteristically, Frith quickly spotted the opportu-nity to create a new business as a specialist publish-er of photographs. He lived in an era of immense and sometimes violent change. For the poor in the early part of Victoria's reign work was exhausting and the hours long, and people had precious little free time to enjoy themselves. Most people had no transport other than a cart or gig at their disposal, and rarely

business one only has to look at the catalogue issued by Frith & Co in 1886: it runs to some 670 pages, listing not only many thousands of views of the British Isles but also many photographs of most European countries, and China, Japan, the USA and Canada - note the sample page shown on page 9 from the hand-written Frith & Co ledgers recording the pictures. By 1890 Frith had created the greatest specialist photographic publishing company in the world, with over 2,000 sales outlets - more than the combined number that Boots and WH Smith have today! The picture on the next page shows the Frith & Co display board at Ingleton in the Yorkshire Dales (left of window). Beautifully constructed with a mahogany frame and gilt inserts, it could display up to a dozen local scenes.

POSTCARD BONANZA

The ever-popular holiday postcard we know today took many years to develop. In 1870 the Post Office issued the first plain cards, with a pre-printed stamp on one face. In 1894 they allowed other publishers' cards to be sent through the mail with an attached adhesive halfpenny stamp. Demand grew rapidly, and in 1895 a new size of postcard was permitted called the court card, but there was little room for illustration. In 1899, a year after Frith's death, a new card measuring 5.5 x 3.5 inches became the standard format, but it was not until 1902 that the divided back came into being, so that the address and message could be on one face and a full-size illustration on the other. Frith & Co were in the vanguard of postcard development: Frith's sons Eustace and Cyril continued their father's monumental task, expanding the number of views offered to the public and recording more and more places in Britain, as the coasts and countryside were opened up to mass travel.

Francis Frith had died in 1898 at his villa in Cannes, his great project still growing. The archive he created continued in business for another seventy years. By 1970 it contained over a third of a million pictures showing 7,000 British towns and villages.

travelled far beyond the boundaries of their own town or village. However, by the 1870s the railways had threaded their way across the country, and Bank Holidays and half-day Saturdays had been made obligatory by Act of Parliament. All of a sudden the working man and his family were able to enjoy days out and see a little more of the world.

With typical business acumen, Francis Frith foresaw that these new tourists would enjoy having souvenirs to commemorate their days out. In 1860 he married Mary Ann Rosling and set out on a new career: his aim was to photograph every city, town and village in Britain. For the next thirty years he travelled the country by train and by pony and trap, producing fine photographs of seaside resorts and beauty spots that were keenly bought by millions of Victorians. These prints were painstakingly pasted into family albums and pored over during the dark nights of winter, rekindling precious memories of summer excursions.

THE RISE OF FRITH & CO

Frith's studio was soon supplying retail shops all over the country. To meet the demand he gathered about him a small team of photographers, and published the work of independent artist-photographers of the calibre of Roger Fenton and Francis Bedford. In order to gain some understanding of the scale of Frith's

St Catherine's College
Senate House & Library
Gerrard Hostel Bridge
Geological Museum
Addenbrooke's Hospital
St Mary's Church
Fitzwilliam Museum, Pitt Press &c
Buxton, The Crescent
  "   The Colonnade
  "   Public Gardens
Haddon Hall, View from the Terrace
Millers Dale
Bakewell, Bridge &c
  "   Footbridge
  "   Church
  "   " Interior
Matlock Bath, The High Tor
  "   On the Derwent
  "   " Brunswood Terrace
  "   Cliff &c

FRANCIS FRITH'S LEGACY

Frith's legacy to us today is of immense significance and value, for the magnificent archive of evocative photographs he created provides a unique record of change in the cities, towns and villages throughout Britain over a century and more. Frith and his fellow studio photographers revisited locations many times down the years to update their views, compiling for us an enthralling and colourful pageant of British life and character.

We are fortunate that Frith was dedicated to recording the minutiae of everyday life. For it is this sheer wealth of visual data, the painstaking chronicle of changes in dress, transport, street layouts, buildings, housing, engineering and landscape that captivates us so much today. His remarkable images offer us a powerful link with the past and with the lives of our ancestors.

THE VALUE OF THE ARCHIVE TODAY

Computers have now made it possible for Frith's many thousands of images to be accessed almost instantly. Frith's images are increasingly used as visual resources, by social historians, by researchers into genealogy and ancestry, by architects and town planners, and by teachers involved in local history projects.

In addition, the archive offers every one of us an opportunity to examine the places where we and our families have lived and worked down the years. Highly successful in Frith's own era, the archive is now, a century and more on, entering a new phase of popularity. Historians consider the Francis Frith Collection to be of prime national importance. It is the only archive of its kind remaining in private ownership. Francis Frith's archive is now housed in an historic timber barn in the beautiful village of Teffont in Wiltshire. Its founder would not recognize the archive office as it is today. In place of the many thousands of dusty boxes containing glass plate negatives and an all-pervading odour of photographic chemicals, there are now ranks of computer screens. He would be amazed to watch his images travelling round the world at unimaginable speeds through internet lines.

The archive's future is both bright and exciting. Francis Frith, with his unshakeable belief in making photographs available to the greatest number of people, would undoubtedly approve of what is being done today with his lifetime's work. His photographs depicting our shared past are now bringing pleasure and enlightenment to millions around the world a century and more after his death.

HERTFORDSHIRE
AN INTRODUCTION

ONE hundred and fifty years or so before Frith's photographer took the photographs in this book, Charles Lamb wrote: 'Slow journeying on to the green plains of Hertfordshire'. By the 1960s slow journeys were a thing of the past, and the county was criss-crossed by a network of roads and railways. New towns, larger than Lamb would have though possible, had sprung up and new industries, of whose nature Lamb could never have dreamed, had become established. Nevertheless, the green plains survived, and were still protected from the north winds by the gentle uplands of the eastern reaches of the Chilterns. Whilst the main routes were becoming steel and concrete, the country roads remained leafy back-ways where little had changed.

Fifty years after the Frith photographer photographed Hertfordshire, the county is cleaved by motorways and high speed railway lines - only the meandering rivers and canals in the extreme east

KINGS LANGLEY, *The Ovaltine Factory c1965* K95056

and west appear unchanged, although the commercial trade has all but disappeared from them, and its place has been taken by recreational and pleasure craft. The new towns of Stevenage, Hatfield and Hemel Hempstead, built to accommodate the London overspill, grew from small market towns. In the 1950s and 1960s they were considered to offer desirable and attractive homes away from the polluted air of the capital. Nothing is new - in the mid 1800s, a correspondent to 'Notes and Queries' said: 'They who buy houses in Hertfordshire pay three quarters purchase for the air.' Those people moving to Hertfordshire in the 1950s would certainly have agreed.

Away from these overspill towns, a journey by car or on foot can be rewarding. The scenery varies from the modern garden cities such as Letchworth and Welwyn to the traditional sleepy villages of Westmill and Bovingdon. The traveller may pass the walls of proud castles, stately mansions, medieval churches and Roman remains - all pronouncing the varied fortunes and history of Hertfordshire. A gentle tour brings us into contact with all manner of intriguing corners of the county.

We might start our journey at Tring, on the Roman Akeman Street in the far north west, where the Natural History Museum's zoological collection is housed; then to Water End, near Gaddesden, with its world-famous watercress beds on the River Gade; and then southwards to Berkhamsted and the remains of its ancient castle close to the Grand Union Canal. East along the Grand Union is Hemel Hempstead, a typical 1950s/60s new town developed out of an old market centre. On the eastern border, close to Buckinghamshire, lies Bovingdon and its Second

World War airfield. Bovingdon boasts of its Dock because villagers thought that the pond was so large that ocean-going liners could dock in the centre of their village. After stopping at other villages and towns along our route, we would find ourselves at Boreham Wood, just off the A1 Barnet by-pass road, a constantly developing town and home to the Albert Square of 'Eastenders' and the underground headquarters of many of James Bond's adversaries. The tradition of filming at Elstree thrives in the studios and huge sets which have moved to Boreham Wood (or should we call it, as the railway station suggests, Borehamwood?) St Albans provides us with a cathedral, a Roman town, a market and a centre for industry and education. Here, just off the M10, layer upon layer of civilisation can be peeled back to give us an insight into the lifestyle of our earlier ancestors.

Moving to the east of Hertfordshire, where barley, its main product, was converted into malt and ale, the towns and villages are strung along the River Lee. Ware, Hoddesdon and Stansted Abbots were known as 'the cradle of the malting industry in England'. Today, these towns are no longer involved in the malting industry, but the communications systems survive in the A10 road linking London to Royston and on to Cambridge. The soil here is ideal for cereal production, and reinforced the county's reputation as a granary area. The villages became affluent from the coaching trade and from wheat production, where the profits paid for fine churches to be built in villages such as Hunsdon, Much Hadham and Standon.

Our journey would take us northwards next, close to the eastern border along the route of the lost railway line between Ware and Buntingford, through Standon, home to the Three Bears, and Braughing with its deserted Roman town. Here we cross Ermine Street and arrive at Westmill, one of the most photographed villages in Hertfordshire. This is a fine place to rest for refreshment at the traditional tearooms or the interestingly named Sword in Hand pub; we might take the chance to stroll to Button Snap in Cherry Green, the house once owned, but not occupied, by Charles Lamb.

Back on the road, our next stopping place would be Buntingford and its long, straight High Street, the old Roman Ermine Street. Don't rely on the time recorded by the town clock above the shops in the High Street - it only has an hour hand! Drive down the cobbled Church Street and along the valley of the River Rib, through the sleepy village of Wyddial and onto the B1368 at the intriguingly named Cave Gate. It is said that a tunnel leads from the cottage to nearby Anstey Castle (worth a visit but don't expect battlements - just a mound with a huge moat teeming with fish); but the truth is that Cave Gate was a mine providing chalk for 'marling' the clayey soil. Swing northwards past Biggin, once an outlying branch of the hospital at Hitchin, which provided rest for travellers and isolation for those suffering from unfortunate diseases! We continue on through Barkway with its fine school founded in 1839 and its unusual milestone.

The route forks to Royston, home of the lost priory (only a few fragments survive), and, if you choose a summer Sunday, it is worthwhile seeking out the unique Royston Cave close to the traffic lights. It is said to have been dug by the Templars; to have been used to store butter at the market; or to have been home to a hermit - take your choice, but don't miss the opportunity to visit the cave!

Royston stands at the crossing of the Icknield Way and the Roman Ermine Street. Follow the road westwards taken by our ancestors, the Icknield, and cross the parallel 1850s railway to Ashwell to visit the beautiful medieval church. Here graffiti record the terrible waves of plagues and natural tragedies that hit the village through the years. We go back along the Icknield to Baldock, a Roman town which later, it is said, was held by the Knights Templar, who named it after Baghdad; and then on through the village of Norton, where the school was once in a pub, and into Ebenezer Howard's Letchworth Garden City. Following the Chiltern ridge along the

KINGS LANGLEY, *The Grand Union Canal c1965* K95073

Icknield brings us to Hitchin, split by the River Hiz and home to the unique British Schools Museum. It holds the country's best collection of objects relating to the history of education, and includes a reconstructed classroom based on the Lancastrian monitoral system of teaching.

Driving southwards, we would come to the 'sleepy little village' of Kimpton, where every year a May Queen is chosen to parade along the High Street to be crowned on the village green, and then to Codicote, where one of the residents managed to be buried twice in the same grave! We go on to Ayot, home of George Bernard Shaw; Wheathampstead, home of the Cherry-Garrard family, one of whose sons travelled with Scott to the South Pole; Harpenden, home of the late Eric Morecambe; and Redbourn, home of Dr Stephens of ink fame. We continue through the large towns: St Albans, where there once was a sophisticated telegraph system, Hatfield, where the cub-reporter Charles Dickens wrote about a tragic fire, and Hertford, the county town and home of McMullens' Brewery.

Finally, we head northwards across the tree-lined open spaces of Welwyn Garden City to Digswell, the site of a horrendous railway fire during the 19th century. Then we reach Watton-at-Stone, so-called because of the two large lumps of Hertfordshire pudding-stone standing at the north end of the village, Datchworth, the most haunted village in Hertfordshire, Knebworth, home of the Lytton family, Bennington, with its 'Lordship', and into Old Stevenage, which even today retains its traditional atmosphere. The last village on our tour will be Walkern, home of the alleged witch Joan Wenham. When you have toured the village, drop into the friendly Yew Tree pub and reflect that during your journey round Hertfordshire you have not used a motorway, ridden on a train nor 'sailed' aboard a narrow boat.

Hertfordshire may be a county of busy roads, but its beauty and heritage live on if you search for it. The County Council's guide for 1956 said: 'For the rambler there are many pretty, fragrant, shady lanes, far-famed commons, coppices and woods'. Francis Frith's photographers had a keen eye for the best view of a landscape or a building, ancient or modern, and their work encapsulates the county of Hertfordshire that we know and love.

HUNSDON, *The Green 1960* H475005

AROUND HERTFORDSHIRE

TRING

The Parish Church of St Peter and St Paul c1960
T81033

It is thought that there has been a building on the site of the church since Roman times. A coin of Emperor Constantine, c337AD, was found on the site close to the line of the old Akeman Street and its crossing with the Icknield Way. The corbels on the arches of the nave are worth a close examination. They depict a pig wearing a friar's cowl; a fox running off with a goose; and a monkey in a religious habit carrying a bottle in one hand and a book in the other. The church registers record the baptisms of a number of the early members of the family of George Washington, first President of the United States of America.

TRING, *The Zoological Museum c1955* T81028

The museum was erected in 1881 as a 21st birthday present for Walter Rothschild by his mother at a cost of £3300. It was designed by William Huckville, and built by the local builders J Honour & Sons; it replaced the original museum in a shed at the bottom of the garden! The museum was opened to the public in 1892, and attracted over 30,000 visitors each year. When Walter Rothschild died in 1939, the collection and museum were passed to the Natural History Museum, in whose possession they remain today.

WATER END *c1955* W547001

Close to the village of Nettleden is one of the most beautiful places in the county. At Water End, the River Gade runs under the fine three-arched bridge and through water meadows shaded by beech, willow and oak trees. One early visitor recorded in her journal: 'Water End, where the broad pool of the river is shaded by large trees.'

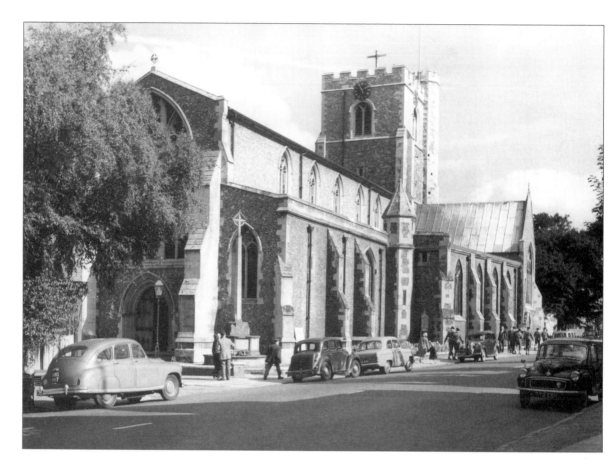

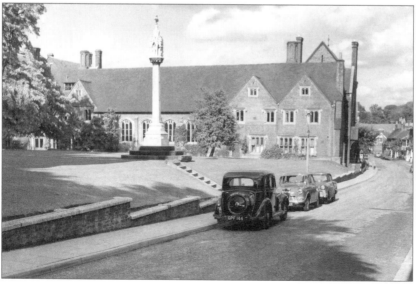

◄ **BERKHAMSTED**
School House c1960
B407047

Parked by the side of Kings Road and opposite the memorial are a gleaming black Rover 14, a Riley 1.5 and an early F-type Vauxhall Victor. The school in the background was founded in 1541 by John Incent, Dean of St Paul's, to provide education for 144 boys. Work was completed in 1544, and the school has been in continuous use since then. William Camden, the antiquarian, said: 'This fine old school building is the only structure in Berkhamsted worth a second glance.'

BERKHAMSTED
*The Parish Church
c1955* B407044

The parish church of St Peter, which dates from before 1222, was built on the site of part of the old St John's Chapel at the side of the Roman Akeman Street. In 1870 it was restored and clad in faced flint to a design by William Butterfield. The surplus flints from the interior were saved and used to build Sunnyside Church of St Michael and All Angels, which was dedicated in June 1909. Among the treasures of St Peter's is a window commemorating the Hertfordshire poet William Cowper, who was born at Berkhamsted Rectory in 1731.

▲ **BERKHAMSTED,** *Ashlyns School c1955* B407039

Ashlyns School was built in 1933-35 and accepted its first pupils in September 1935. It originally offered places for 400 pupils aged between 5 and 15 years. The site had been used as an overflow for Thomas Coram's Bloomsbury Foundling Hospital, but had passed to the estate of nearby Ashlyns Hall prior to its purchase in 1929. The new school was inaugurated by Prince Arthur of Connaught in July 1935; it became a Secondary Modern School in January 1951. Amongst its treasures were the original coat of arms from Coram's Hospital, which still forms part of the pediment, and an organ donated by G F Handel to the Foundling Hospital. Unfortunately, the organ was removed when the County Council completed the purchase of the school in 1955.

◀ **BERKHAMSTED**
*The High Street and the Parish
Church c1955* B407003

As late as 1930, parts of the High Street at Berkhamsted were not fully made up; but with the increase of traffic on this main arterial road, it had one of the first junctions in Hertfordshire to become controlled by traffic lights. Pilkingtom Manor, mostly hidden by the trees on the left, was demolished in 1959, and today only the Dower House (the white gabled building in the centre of the photograph) survives. In the early 1800s, Berkhamsted was renowned for its high quality bobbin lace. There was a resurgence of the industry in the early 1900s, but with the importation of the cheaper 'Maltese Pattern' lace, the industry faded and disappeared.

▼ **BOVINGDON,** *High Street, The Ryder Memorial c1965* B409012

The memorial was built in 1881 as a protection over the village well. The main benefactor was Granville Dudley Ryder. A few years later, piped water came to the villages and the well became redundant; by 1908 it had fallen into disrepair. Suggestions were made that it should be moved to another site or even demolished, but local opinion was opposed to any such possibilities. In 1949, a London Transport bus ran into the memorial and achieved the latter proposal. However, it was rebuilt in 1952 at a cost to LTE of £145. The Bell public house (right) dates from the 18th century. In the 1920s, Arthur Lake was the landlord - he was a familiar sight pushing his hand-cart from Hemel Hempstead, where he collected the spirits for sale at the Bell.

▶ **BOVINGDON,** *High Street c1965* B409008

As early as 1943, the parish council discussed the issue of whether Bovingdon would continue as a village or develop into a commercial or industrial area. By 1945, preparations were in hand to 'redevelop and enhance' the village and to build new houses in the surrounding locality. A three-fold increase in the number of children attending the school demonstrated the need for these developments. It remains to be seen if the developers have 'enhanced' the beauty of Bovingdon.

◄ **HEMEL HEMPSTEAD**
Rock and Roll Statue and Water Garden c1960 H255041

Mills and rows of cheap housing were swept away during the development of Marlowes in the new town of Hemel Hempstead. The towpaths of the River Gade, which ran behind Marlowes, were converted into quiet riverside walks and pleasure gardens designed by Sir Geoffrey Jellicoe, with fountains and bronze statues; this photograph shows 'Rock and Roll' sculpted by Hubert Yencesse, a French artist, and installed during the summer of 1962. A copy of 'Rock and Roll' was cast in early 1970 and presented to one of the Australian new towns.

► **HEMEL HEMPSTEAD**
Stoneycroft Shopping Centre, Warners End c1965 H255064

Stoneycroft was part of the new town development, and work started in 1952. The Top of the World pub (left), named after Hilary and Tensing's successful conquering of Mount Everest in 1953, was opened just in time for Christmas 1956. The shops - Constables, Barkers, Kayes, 'Reliable Fruiterers' and Wallaces - have today been replaced by, amongst others, the ubiquitous Chinese takeaway food outlet and charity shops.

▶ **HEMEL HEMPSTEAD**
Marlowes c1965
H255046

Originally a tree lined thoroughfare, Marlowes when it was developed in the early 1950s became the main shopping centre for the new town. Well known chain stores were strongly represented in Marlowes and Bridge Street - Truform Shoes, Dorothy Perkins, Milletts and Burton the tailors were here - as well as local shops and retail outlets such as Vanity Fair and Hiltons. The per annum rentals on these new premises ranged from £1000 to £1500 and £600 to £800 in 1954.

◀ **HEMEL HEMPSTEAD**
The Pavilion and the Odeon Cinema c1965 H255150

The foundation stone of the new Odeon Cinema was laid in 1959 by the actress Lauren Bacall. When the work was completed, the opening ceremony was carried out by the British character actor Leslie Phillips. The Pavilion (centre) offered 'Dancing every Saturday', and local teenagers were entertained by popular music groups such as The Kinks and their lead singer, Ray Davies. In the last few years, the cost of running the Pavilion has been prohibitive, and this once-proud venue has now been demolished.

▲**KINGS LANGLEY,** *The Grand Union Canal c1965* K95073

This cruising converted narrow boat on the Grand Union was photographed a few months before the final northbound commercial operation: early in 1966, Roses Lime Juice sent their final cargo to the wharf at Two Waters, Hemel Hempstead. Southbound transport survived for a few more years and came to an end in 1972, when a Blue Line narrow boat docked at Dickenson's wharf at Croxley Green.

◄**KINGS LANGLEY**
The Village Pound c1960
K95053

The pound has had a chequered career. In 1835 it was moved from its position near the Workhouse, but it has now been rebuilt in its original site opposite Pound Cottages in Common Lane to the north east of the town. The pound was a very necessary community facility. Overseen by the pindar, stray animals were kept here until the owners arrived to pay a small fee for their release. The equivalent today would be the parking clamp and council vehicle pound!

21

KINGS LANGLEY
All Saints' Church c1955
K95020

All Saints' was unique in its having permission to fly the Royal Standard on selected dates and to commemorate royal birthdays and marriages. Unfortunately, this privilege was rescinded around 1925. The structure dates from the 15th century and contains the tomb of Edmund de Langley, the first Duke of York, Earl of Cambridge and fifth son of Edward III. This had originally been installed in the nearby priory chapel of the Friars Preachers, but was moved to All Saints' in 1575.

KINGS LANGLEY, *The Ovaltine Factory c1965* K95056

Wander's Ovaltine Company had been a major employer in Kings and Abbots Langley, but its closure in the 1970s was a major blow to the twin communities. The frontage of this magnificent factory building was saved, and new dwellings have been built to the rear.

KINGS LANGLEY
The High Street c1955
K95023

When Frith's photographer visited Kings Langley in the 1890s, cattle wandered freely along the High Street; but by 1955, the motor car was firmly established as king of the road. He would have recognised the shops, particularly Coles the draper (left), which had been owned by Grays but was taken by Miss Florence Cole in 1911. Next door, in 1893, the newsagent's shop was held by the Rev Daniel Macmillan, Baptist minister of Kings Langley.

KINGS LANGLEY, *The High Street c1965* K95070

The driver of the Ford 300E van in the foreground has popped into Haywood's (right) for his morning newspaper. Next door is Sketchley's, the dry-cleaners, and Arthur Rickett. The imposing brick building beyond was, as many local children will remember, the dentist's surgery. On the opposite side are the opticians, then the baker and Lloyds Bank. Ampleforth's Garage, Austin/Morris main dealers, had been Amos Young's cycle repair work shops - he was also one of the town's tailors! When Ampleforth's moved to other premises, this became The Age of Wine.

23

ABBOTS LANGLEY, *The Ovaltine Dairies c1960* A150030 (top)
ABBOTS LANGLEY, *The Ovaltine Farm c1960* A150049 (above)

In 1865, George Wander, a Swiss chemist, devised a new malted barley nutritional drink called Ovaltine. The company bought Parsonage Farm at Abbots Langley and Numbers Farm at Kings Langley in the 1900s, and the Ovaltine model farm was established at Langley in 1929. It was modelled on the farm created by Louis XIV for Marie Antoinette. By the 1950s, Ovaltine employed 1,400 staff at Langley - the lives of few local people were not influenced by the company or its suppliers. The poultry farm kept one of the largest flocks of laying poultry - over 50,000 White Leghorns - whilst the dairy farm at Bedmond Road boasted a herd of prize-winning pedigree Jersey cattle. By the late 1960s, demand for the product had dropped and parts of the farm had fallen into disrepair; in 1975, the 185ft Ovaltine chimney, which had been built using a quarter of million bricks for £7000, was demolished at a cost of £8000.

ABBOTS LANGLEY
Causeway Parade c1960 A150028

The Causeway development, carried out between 1955 and 1957, created a parade of shops, flats and dwellings on the site of Causeway House, which was finally demolished in 1957. It was built in 1720, and until 1857 had been owned by Miss Caroline Henty, the niece of the Edwardian boy's adventure story writer, G A Henty. The first occupiers of the shops when they opened in 1958 were Mr Hall, consulting optician, Davis TV and radio sales, Christy's gentlemen's and children's outfitters, and Mrs S Henderson, ladies' hairdresser. The timber-faced building in the distance was the local dental practice.

ABBOTS LANGLEY, *Breakspear College, c1960* A150037

Originally known as Langley House, this was the home of Robert Henty, brother of G A Henty and of Lord Kindersley, Director of the Bank of England. In 1928 the Salvatorian Fathers of Wealdstone bought Langley House, and part of it became the Roman Catholic church for the area. By 1930, a school had been established in the stables under Sisters Claudia and Ellidia. It was known as Breakspear College in memory of Nicholas Breakspear, Pope Adrian IV, who was born at Abbots Langley. The property was sold in 1986 to Dr John Munro, who converted it into an allergy clinic. Today it is empty and boarded up, awaiting planning permission for the main house to be broken up into individual dwellings.

WATFORD, *The Town Hall c1955* W40023

The Town Hall was designed by C Cowles-Voysey, and building was completed in 1939. The acoustics in the main assembly hall, on the left, were so good that it was used by gramophone companies for recording classical music performances. During May 1943, the Lancaster bomber which had been exhibited at Trafalgar Square as part of Wings Week was brought to Watford and displayed on the grass frontage of the Town Hall.

WATFORD
The High Street c1955 W40019

Daniel Defoe wrote: 'Watford - the town is very long having but one street'. A few roads had been added during the following three hundred years, but the main High Street is still very long and busy. On the left, standing proudly above the other roofs, is Fisher's butchers shop. In 1881, Francis Fisher had the cottages on the site demolished and erected this imposing new shop. Further on stands the Rose and Crown and the Compasses public houses. Opposite is Cawdells' department store with its imposing 1930s frontage; demonstrating the commercial success and wealth of Watford are branches of the National Provincial, Barclays and Lloyds Banks.

WATFORD, *The High Street c1959* W40051

Cawdells' department store is executing a pincer movement on Timothy Whites, the chemist (left). Beyond comes the pillared portico of the Midland Bank, followed by Lennards and the Pearl Assurance office (later Habitat). The next building is Kingham's store, soon after the photograph was taken to be demolished and replaced by British Home Stores. In the left foreground is Lloyds Bank, originally built in 1889 for the Bucks and Oxon Bank. Today, although the front remains unaltered, the interior has been improved following major renovation in 1983 for Lloyds. Cawdells itself was demolished around 1968.

WATFORD
The Pond, High Street c1955 W40044

This motor historian's delight contains many cars and vans typical of its date. Two Standard Vanguards, a Riley 1½, a Rover 14, a fine Austin Atlantic, an Austin A30 and a Morris J2 van demonstrate the growing traffic problem in Watford town centre. The parade of shops and the Art Deco Odeon cinema (originally the Plaza) on the right were built in 1929. The next showing on the Odeon's new wide screen of 'Suddenly' starring Frank Sinatra is to take place at 1pm. Rivalled and outlived by the Gaumont, which closed in 1983, the Odeon was demolished a few years later, in 1963, to make way for a supermarket.

WATFORD, *The Pond, High Street c1955* W40056

The pond had been a popular watering place for horses, particularly during the Great War when Watford experienced considerable troop movements. Although earlier it had been a wagon-wash, the cleaning of horse-drawn vehicles was strictly prohibited, and railings were erected in 1915 to prevent access. In the 1960s, the Town Council tabled a number of proposals for the development of the Pond, including grassing over the area and installing two concrete grazing horses!

CHORLEYWOOD
Canal Side Cottages c1960
C226025

At the time of this photograph, it appeared that the canal network was moving towards a final decline. However, the owners were justified in their optimism; for the Grand Union Canal and the River Chess, although they see little commercial traffic, are popular with pleasure craft owners. The well-kept towpath and the sympathetic cottage extension we see here blend into the countryside, and in 1960 were prepared for the resurrection of Hertfordshire's waterways.

CHORLEYWOOD, *The Church and the School 1959* C226015

We are looking northwards across the common, where the shingle-clad spire of Christ Church dominates the skyline. The much-respected Christ Church C of E School, founded in 1853, stands in the middle distance. The common covers 200 acres, and was a popular stopping place for drovers on their way to market - here the cattle could be watered by the four ponds. Today, the common abounds with wildlife and makes a colourful asset to the village.

RICKMANSWORTH
The High Street c1955
R33026

Photographed before its conversion to a one-way system, the High Street appears a quiet market town thoroughfare. On the right, the postman delivers the mail to the Automobile Association agent from his wicker handcart. A few doors away, the Swan Hotel has lost the bunch of grapes which, from the time of the Skidmores who owned it from 1692-1820, hung from the hook on the extreme end of the wrought iron inn sign. Some inns displayed a wheatsheaf to inform customers that a new brew of beer was ready for consumption; the Swan hung the grapes to tell patrons that it was open for business.

RICKMANSWORTH, *St Mary's Church and Church Street c1960* R33039

Only the tower survives of the original church. The building was rebuilt and restored on a number of occasions, first in 1630 and later in 1870 to a plan by Blomfield. The east window was designed by Burne-Jones and installed in 1891. Church Street was always liable to flooding, and in March 1947 the water flowed into the lower floor of the Feathers (right). The banks of the nearby river were strengthened, so that today it is safe to drink in the Feathers without wearing waders.

RICKMANSWORTH
Church Street 1952 R33027

With St Mary's Church in the distance, Church Street is typical of a market town by-way in the early 1950s. Barrett & Sons, bakers, proudly advertise that they sell Hovis bread (left), and the Kings Arms public house that it serves Benskins bitter (centre right). The Chequers (left) has become a tea rooms, whilst next door the North Metro Engineering Works provide service for all kinds of motor vehicles. However, although there are many bicycles and a horse-drawn cart in full view, the only motor car is a Standard Vanguard peeping round the far end of the street.

RICKMANSWORTH, *The Railway Station from the Cross Roads c1960* R33043

The last steam train ran through Rickmansworth on 9 September 1961, when the newly electrified extension was opened through to Aylesbury. The Baker Street to Rickmansworth line had already been electrified using the London Transport Underground network in January 1925 as part of the programme to promote the new villages and towns of Metroland.

RICKMANSWORTH
The High Street c1960
R33028
Fletchers and Woolworth's (left) have been built on the site of the Queen's Arms public house and the old Fotherley Almshouses, which had been erected in 1682 to provide for five poor widows of the town. Woolworth's, which had been opened on 9 March 1934, was closed in 1971, and the property was converted into a supermarket.

▼ **RICKMANSWORTH,** *The High Street c1960* R33035

H P Farr, watchmaker and jeweller, took over the premises on the right shortly after the end of the Second World War, and he remained here until the mid 1960s. Next door was Beesley's Florists, earlier Bell's the tobacconist's, until it was replaced by John's Boutique. Then came Mrs Gristwood's bakery shop, which was replaced by Howe & Son, and ultimately by Spurriers. Further on is the Rickmansworth branch of the National Provincial Bank, which replaced Eastman's butcher shop and the Royal Herts Laundry.

▶ **RICKMANSWORTH**
The Splash, Bury Road c1958 R33032

One of the best-recognised beauty spots in Rickmansworth, the Splash (the town ditch), which is being crossed by the Austin A40, had originally been part of the drive to Bury Manor House, whose gates can be seen in the far distance. By the late 1700s, it was in general use by the public. In the 1960s, icy conditions made the road dangerous to motors, and in August 1963 the road was covered over and a culvert was built.

◄ BUSHEY
The High Street
c1955 B414010

On the left stands Barclays Bank. This was built around 1905 on the site of the London and South West Bank, which in turn had replaced a Tudor farm house. The High Street was the main road from London to Birmingham, and a toll gate was erected in 1769. This continued to operate until 1872. On the right, close to the tail of the sleek American Plymouth car, is a small green on which stood the village pump. As it was close to the graveyard, the local people used to comment that they were 'drinking their ancestors in solution'.

GARSTON
The Manor Works Assessment Shop c1955 G307011

In 1931, the widow of Stafford Bourne (the son of one of the founders of Bourne & Hollingsworth's store in London) sold Garston Manor to Benskins the brewers, who transferred it to the North West Metropolitan Regional Hospital Board. The Board converted the manor into a medical rehabilitation centre to accommodate men and women between the ages of sixteen and seventy who were recovering from physical disabilities resulting from injury or illness.

BOREHAMWOOD
The Church of St Michael and All Angels c1965 B408035

The foundation stone was laid in October 1954 by the late Princess Margaret and blessed by the Lord Bishop of St Albans. St Michael's was built to provide a church for the rapidly expanding town of Borehamwood. The bell came from the mortuary chapel at Ayot St Peter, to whom it had been donated by Charles Willes Wilshere of The Frythe in 1876.

POTTERS BAR, *Wyllyotts Manor, the Council Offices 1966* P131037

This part 16th-century timber-framed building is named after the Wylyot or Williot family, who held the manor in the mid 1300s as an outlier of the manor of South Mimms. The property was once owned by Alderman James Hickson, a city brewer, who left it to the Brewers' Company to support six almshouses in South Mimms. In 1966, the complex was wholly occupied as council offices, but today it contains a restaurant and a cinema. Also on the site stands the fine museum of the Potters Bar and District Historical Society which was opened in 1990.

POTTERS BAR, *Oakmere House and the Lake c1966* P131015

Built around 1800, the original Oakmere House was destroyed by fire whilst being extended. The new building was occupied in the period leading up to the Great War by the Forbes family; Eileen Baillie recalls old Mrs E M Forbes 'lying on an elegant couch ... having her beautiful hair dressed by her maid in a silvery crown over her head'. The winters during the Great War were particularly cold, and when the lake froze over Mrs Forbes gave permission for the local people to skate there. In 1916, the L31 Zeppelin was shot down and crashed in the farm estate of

Oakmere House. The local people rushed to the house and woke Mrs Forbes, who appeared at the door in her night clothes. The excited people told her what had happened; but annoyed at being woken, she replied, 'All right, we will see to it in the morning!' and slammed the door in their faces. Parts of the Zeppelin can be seen in Potters Bar's fine museum at the Wyllyotts Centre. In the 1980s, Oakmere House was converted to a Beefeater restaurant.

POTTERS BAR, *Mutton Lane and Darkes Lane c1960* P131034

This is now a busy junction close to the shopping centre; this photograph gives no clue to the traffic jams that were to become so familiar in the near future. The pedestrians can safely cross the road without special signals - the traffic lights seem almost redundant. The M25 is still a pipe dream in the minds of the planners, but already the town has begun to develop. Local stores such as Barkhams, Kirschels and Walkers (centre and right) will soon be joined by branches of the major supermarket chains.

◀ **CHESHUNT,** *Temple Bar, Theobalds Park c1955*
C319024

Designed by Christopher Wren in 1672 as a triumphal arch, Temple Bar originally stood at the top of Fleet Street in London. In 1878, it was removed because it was proving to be a major restriction to traffic. When the Meux family brought the remains to Theobalds, they had intended that it should become the gate-house to the estate, but it was never properly installed. Over the years there have been a number of attempts to return Temple Bar to London, but it seems that each proposal is blocked by bureaucracy.

POTTERS BAR
The Church of the Vincentian Spanish Fathers c1965 P131048

In 1922 the Vincentian Spanish fathers acquired a plot of land at Hillside in Barnet Road to provide a training facility for young priests to foreign missions. The new building was completed in 1925, but it was destroyed by a V2 rocket in 1945. Several people were killed, and much damage was done to local property. In 1960 a new church, designed by Felix Velerde, was built at a cost of £40,000 and dedicated to St Vincent de Paul and St Louis de Marillac.

▲ **CHESHUNT,** *The Public Library c1955* C319025

The library, part funded by a gift to the people of Cheshunt by the Andrew Carnegie Foundation, was opened to the public in 1907. Designed by J Myrtle Smith, the library included a School of Art. Every detail in the building was crafted with a meticulous eye for design; the banisters on the stairs, the handles to the doors, the stained glass windows, all were manufactured for this specific building and to the highest possible standard. The first Librarian was Oswald C Hudson. He was given a magnificent annual grant of £14 to purchase new books. Such was the demand from the expanding population that new wings were added (after this photograph was taken) in 1956.

◄ **CHESHUNT**
Grundy Park, c1955
C319001

Originally one of the largest country houses in the town of Cheshunt, Grundy Park is now home to one of the Borough of Broxbourne's leisure centres. The grounds are still attractive quiet public gardens, but the fine topiary has disappeared. The greenhouses on the right provided particularly fine blossoms throughout the year and were in great demand during civic gatherings.

▶ **CHESHUNT**
Turner's Hill c1965
C319050

Newnham Parade, built in the early 1960s on the site of the old Triangle Cafe (which had been demolished in 1960), was a favourite meeting place for locals and travellers from London to Ware. In the 1990s the fountain was the subject of occasional comment by residents, who complained that the water height was not quite up to standard. An officer of the local council was deputised to be 'Fountain Monitor' to record the force each day. In winter, when the fountain froze, this was a particularly challenging responsibility.

◀ **TURNFORD**
The High Road c1965
T158001

Many of the houses along the High Road at Turnford were built to accommodate the workers on the nearby market gardens. On the centre left, in the far distance, is a garage. A few years before the time of this photograph its yard had been filled with derelict cars, and it was a popular scavenging ground for spare parts. The writer bought a Ford V8 Pilot here, and ran it for a number of years using second-hand parts extracted, with some difficulty and hazard, from the mounds of abandoned vehicles.

43

BROXBOURNE
St Augustine's Church
c1955 B413008

The town of Broxbourne runs along the old north road, and was originally one of the largest parishes in the county. Hoddesdon was a small hamlet on its northern boundary, but when its church of St Paul was built, it broke away. Today, the upstart Hoddesdon is a large and successful market town, whilst Broxbourne boasts only a short row of shops in its High Street. Broxbourne's parish church of St Augustine is much larger than St Paul's. It

contains a number of interesting monuments, including a memorial to the Scottish road engineer, John Louden Macadam, who lived at Hoddesdon, and Edward Christian, brother of Fletcher Christian who led the mutiny on the 'Bounty'.

BROXBOURNE, *St Augustine's Church and the New River c1955* B413013

The New River, whose source is at Amwell Springs, was built at the orders of Sir Hugh Myddleton to supply clean water to London. John Macadam, who is remembered in the church, once employed a local man, George Allen, to manufacture an iron ring. If a stone passed through the ring, it was the correct size for road building. Allen asked Macadam what would happen if the ring was ever lost. 'Why, George', replied Macadam, 'let them try the pieces in their mouths. If they go in, they will be small enough'.

BROXBOURNE
The River Lea 1960
B413032

The River Lea, part of the Leesic Navigation, runs for a long distance parallel to the New River. Pleasure boats could be hired for trips and picnics on the river bank, and further north, Rye House was a popular weekend venue for east Londoners seeking respite from the smoky capital. The boathouse photographed here on the Essex/Hertfordshire border lies close to the interestingly named Carthegena Lock.

HODDESDON, *The High Street c1960* H259046

Standing in the High Street at Hoddesdon must be one of the last horse-drawn milk delivery floats in the district (centre right). Just beyond is the Bull Hotel (demolished 1964), whose original sign spanned the whole of the High Street and proved a trial to drivers perched high on their wagons. On the same side are two more public houses which had served the thirsty farmers attending the busy cattle market opposite. It is said that in the 1830s, Hoddesdon supported 28 inns.

HODDESDON
The High Street c1960
H259047

The Standard Vanguard and the police motorcycle stand outside what is now the Roman Catholic Church of St Augustine and the junction with Charlton Way. On the right, the two Ford Populars and the Morris Eight Series 1 tourer are parked outside the Home and Colonial Stores (now a pizza parlour and a video hire shop) and the block of three chain shops - William Bros (who offered customer loyalty tokens avidly collected by children), F W Woolworth and Timothy Whites & Taylors. Today they are an Indian restaurant, a bedding store and the mouth-watering Taste of China restaurant. The London to Ware single-decker bus is about to stop outside the Golden Lion - a cosy timber framed pub with a golden glowing interior lit with real fires and offering fine beers. No need to go hungry in Hoddesdon!

HODDESDON
The Tower Centre c1965
H259120

The centre of Hoddesdon suffered major changes during the 1960s. The Bull was demolished in 1964, and at the same time the Maidenhead Inn was swept away to make way for the Tower Centre, which was opened in 1967. It was never particularly successful, and the main shopping precinct remains rather dingy and damp. The exterior, which appears attractive, modern and bright in 1965, is now looking out of date and tired. It seems that the optimism of the 1960s has given way to a desire to return to the old ways, and the traditional Hoddesdon shops continue to flourish and attract customers from the surrounding villages and communities.

STANSTED ABBOTS, *Easneye Drive c1960* S181002

Originally called Isneye, Easneye was bought by Thomas Fowell Buxton in 1866. A new house was built to a design by Alfred Waterhouse, the architect of St Pancras Station and London's Natural History Museum. Its Gothic exterior is particularly attractive to film makers, and Easneye became St Trinian's School when the stories by Ronald Searle were filmed. Today Easneye is the All Nations College for Missionaries.

GREAT AMWELL, *The Church of St John the Baptist c1955* A155003

The small Norman church at Great Amwell stands close to the New River and contains a memorial to Robert Mylne, one of the engineers to the New River Company. The tower was added to the church in the 15th century, and later this was surmounted by a spire. The village stocks still survive near the church, and so does the pigeon-house to Amwellbury. This was converted to a tasteful dwelling during the 1990s by the Hertfordshire Building Preservation Trust.

49

▶ **GREAT AMWELL**
The New River c1955
A155002

Various schemes had been proposed to bring fresh water to London; it was around 1600 that Edmund Colthurst identified the springs at Chadwell and Amwell as an ideal source. Work began on the New River with funding from Hugh Myddleton in 1610, and despite a number of delays through objections by local landowners, the project was completed within a few years. The photograph shows the idyllic and peaceful scene near the source of the New River, a contrast with its southern end in the bustling capital. The memorial on the right is inscribed with John Scott's words: 'AMWELL! Perpetual be thy stream: Nor e'en thy spring be less: Which thousands drink who never dream: Whence flows the boon they bless'.

◀ **HERTFORD**
The Flower Pot, Maidenhead Street c1950 H77003

The Flower Pot was originally in a building to the right of the present public house. It was first recorded in 1803 as an unlicensed beer house when it was owned by Thomas Driver Metcalf. The new building, with its later fine stained glass windows, was erected in 1886 when the licence was held by Percy Hargreaves.

▲ **HERTFORD,** *County Hall c1955* H77013

In 1935, following their success in an architectural competition, James & Bywater, with Rowland Pierce, oversaw the building of the new County Hall in Peggs Lane. Miskin & Sons were the main contractors, and Bysouth Ltd carried out much of the stonework. The building was completed in 1939.

◄**HERTFORD**
Ware Road c1960 H77046

During the mid 19th century, new suburban houses were built along the road leading to Ware. As well as dwellings, one or two factories provided work for local people. The main employer was Addis, the brush manufacturers, who came to Hertford in the 1920s when they took over the premises of the Hertford Steam Laundry Company. In 1935 they built a new state-of-the-art factory to a design by David Hamilton. Although production has now moved to Wales, the Grade II listed building still survives in Ware Road.

HERTFORD, *Parliament Square c1950* H77002

It is said that Jane Austen based Meryton, in 'Pride and Prejudice', on Hertford, and that Elizabeth Bennet met Mr Darcy at Shire Hall. If this were true, she would have been driven past Parliament Square. However, it would not have been the pleasant, open area photographed by Frith. In 1920 a number of squalid and tightly packed buildings had to be demolished during the construction of the war memorial, which was designed by Sir Aston Webb and sculpted by Alfred Drury. It was unveiled in November 1921.

WARE

Baldock Street c1955 W24001

Baldock Street leads northwards out of Ware towards Thundridge. The higgledy-piggledy row of pubs, shops and dwellings has hardly changed over the years. The driver climbing out of his Morris 8 Series E is parked outside one of the many cafes in Baldock Street (centre right) - this one used to be the Golden Boot public house and sported a giant hanging metal gold-painted knee-boot sign. Next door was the Royston Crow, and opposite was the Bull's Head, which is still open for business today.

◄ **WARE**
Crib Street c1955
W24023

Redevelopment in the 1970s has swept away many of the buildings on the west side of Crib Street. With the wrought iron gate and lantern frame in front of us, we look northwards towards Bourne Close and eventually, by a footpath across the fields, to Moles Farm and the Sow and Pigs public house at Thundridge. The Cabin and the Albion are on the right, whilst in the distance, opposite the almost obscured MG sports car, are the Red Cow and the White Horse.

WARE
The River Lea c1960
W24042

It is difficult to imagine this peaceful river scene as it was only twenty years previously. Then, it was a bustling port with barges moored two or three deep unloading timber and barley. A few more years earlier, there would have been the occasional sailing barge with huge brown sails. During the Second World War, much of London's stock of timber was

moved to the yards at Ware belonging to such companies as Albany and Gluckstein. Commercial barge traffic ceased about 1949, but the river continued (and continues today) to be used for recreational and leisure purposes.

WARE

The High Street c1965
W24073

The south-west side of Ware High Street changed drastically when it was decided to build a new Tesco Store in 1960. The building on the left with the twin flag poles had been Swan & Nickholes, the grocer's, and was rebuilt as the Eastern Electricity Board's showrooms. Long after the Fleur de Luce public house was closed, the site was taken by Jenning & Bewley, printers, and Ware Library - both of these were lost to Tesco, and so was Gideon Talbot's car repair workshop and roadside pavement-mounted petrol pumps. Fortunately, the French Horn public house on the east side of the High Street survived.

◀ **HUNSDON**, *The Green 1960* H475005

The Village Hall at Hunsdon was originally the school until the building of the new school in 1924 at a cost of £4000. Now it is a meeting place for people of all ages from the youngest toddler to the most venerated member of the Over Sixties Club. When Hunsdon won the Hertfordshire Best Kept Village competition in 1960, the winner's sign was erected in the garden of the house next door. Now a quiet, peace-loving village, life is a far cry from 1690, when Moses Dunkley stole a shirt worth 6d and stocking worth 2d here. He was convicted and was 'whipped until his back was bloody' in Angel Inn Yard, Hertford.

WARESIDE
The White Horse c1955
W290005

So often forgotten by travellers through Hertfordshire, Wareside is one of the county's prettiest villages. Situated on the uplands to the south of the River Ash, it straddles the B1004 road between Much Hadham and Ware. Up to the time of Dr Beeching's 'axe', its station at nearby Mardock was served by the single track Buntingford Branch railway line which also ran through the villages of Widford, Hadham, Standon, Braughing and Westmill. Frith's photographer captured views of all these communities, and it seems likely that he rode on the line during his photograph forays. It is said that in the late 1800s Wareside boasted seven public houses; the White Horse and its sister, the Chequers, were the sole survivors in 1955.

▲ **HUNSDON,** *The High Street 1960* H475007

The honour of being entitled Hertfordshire's tidiest village for 1960 went to the village of Hunsdon near Ware. The competition for Best Kept Village was divided into a number of categories - Hunsdon won the prize in the 'Larger Village' section, with Shenley, Welwyn and Potten End, near Hemel following up. This photograph was taken shortly after the winner's sign (left) was installed in the front garden next to the village hall, and it shows how justified the judges were in making the decision. With neat flower beds, carefully trimmed verges and totally litter-free footpaths, Hunsdon was justly proud of its achievement.

◀ **SAWBRIDGEWORTH**
Bell Street c1965 S67022

Leading from the High Street to the Square, Bell Street is lined with shops and public houses. However, if the visitor looks at the upper storeys or, if opportunity presents itself, at the rear elevation of the buildings, they give the clues to their origins. Some of the buildings are a century older than their Georgian frontages, and one is reputed to be haunted by two women dressed in Romany costume. The photograph shows Bell Street as a quiet back street in a small market town with only one car and a solitary cyclist - a far cry from the busy shopping centre of today.

▶ **SAWBRIDGEWORTH**
Knight Street c1965
S67020

The eastern end of Bell Street is crossed by Knight Street, a wide road leading from Station Road to Fair Green where a market and fair have been held since the charter was granted in 1306. On 1 April, and later in October, children would have streamed along Knight Street from the school to buy treacle toffee or sherbet and liquorice straws from Mrs Cockerton. Today, the market which originally covered the Market Square and Fair Green has gone, but each year a few roundabouts and stalls still visit the town.

◀ **SAWBRIDGEWORTH**
Fair Green c1965 S67031

Fair Green lies past the junction of Bell Street and Knight Street and of the site of the town pump. It has an air of quiet elegance in the centre of this bustling town. A plaque dated 22 August 1951 set into the wall of the garden of Corner House reads: 'This plaque was erected by the Sawbridgeworth Urban District to commemorate the transfer to the Council of the manorial rights in the Fair Green, which rights are the subject of a charter granted by King Henry VI on the 13th February 1448'.

▲ **SAWBRIDGEWORTH,** *The River c1965* S67024

The River Stort formed the boundary between Hertfordshire and Essex and provided the transportation service for the malting industry in the town. Today it is mainly used by pleasure craft, although there are plans for some small commercial use. The Stort has its source near Clavering in Essex, and increases in width and becomes navigable at Bishop's Stortford. It flows southwards and eventually empties into the Thames.

◀ **BISHOP'S STORTFORD**
South Street c1955
B104025

Although the B1004 is called the High Street, it is South Street that provides the main shopping centre for the town. In 1955 there were cafes and tea rooms, confectioners and tobacconists, butchers and bakers. Today South Street contains building societies, banks, opticians, mobile 'phone stores and gift shops. Our photograph shows one bus and one bicycle: today it is a nose-to-tail stream of traffic, and strictly no parking.

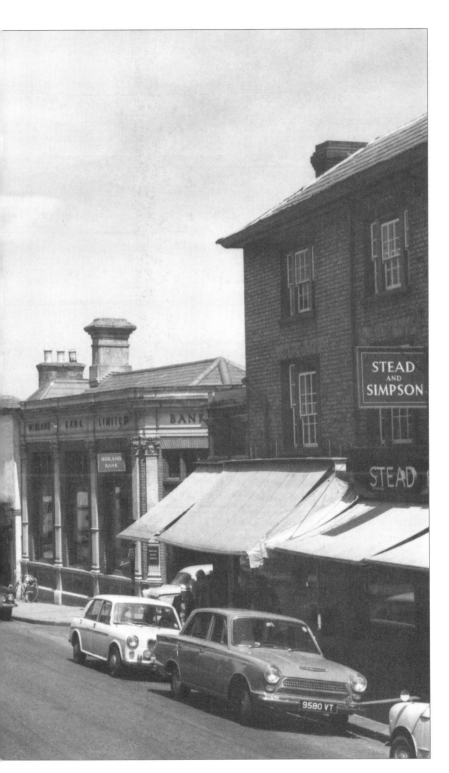

BISHOP'S STORTFORD
North Street c1965
B104075

The Eastern Electricity
Board office occupies the
Old White Horse pub (left).
A typical East Anglian
building with a pargetted
facade made from low relief
design pressed into the wet
mortar, it dates from the
1500s, and contains some
fine interior mouldings.
Although the traffic is light,
an early engraving shows a
busy street choked with
carriages and wagons when
the road was much
narrower and before many
buildings were demolished
for road widening in the
early 1800s.

BISHOP'S STORTFORD
Hockerill Teacher Training College c1960
B104080

The Diocesan Teacher Training College at Hockerill was started by the Rev Menet and the Rev Rhodes in 1852. Some time after the end of the Second World War, it became a boys' boarding school run by Essex County Council. Today, it houses the Hockerill Anglo-European School.

MUCH HADHAM, *Church Lane c1955* M181030

Looking southwards along Church Lane, we see the thatched Glebe Cottage, which was originally two dwellings. Beyond it is Wickham Cottage, which has since undergone major restoration. The furthest building is known today as The Cottage, but village people still remember it as Clements' Cottage. It was here that Mr Clements used to cut men's hair for sixpence, but as local lore has it, 'not the hair of conscientious objectors'.

MUCH HADHAM
St Andrew's Church c1955
M181021

St Andrew's Church stands on the high ground to the west of the River Ash's water meadows. Adjacent, to the north, is the old palace which belonged to the Bishop of London. Some of the windows in the church were designed by Henry Moore, who lived in the nearby hamlet of Perry Green. In 1982, the Anglican congregation combined with the Roman Catholic church of the Holy Cross, and St Andrew's is now run jointly.

STANDON, *The Ford c1965* S377015

A few yards south of the paper mill, the trackway crosses the River Rib through a gently flowing ford. Gently flowing, that is, until the winter showers or the spring sun melts the snow, when the Rib becomes a raging torrent. Many motorists have been caught out and found themselves taking an unexpected route to Standon Lordship and Latchford. The mill was one of the two main Hertfordshire paper works (the other was at Nash and Apsley Mills in the west of the county), but it fell into decline and is now a private residence. Apart from some mechanism, all that remains is Laundry Mead to the left of the view; here, it is said, the rags were hung out to dry before being mashed by the mill's trip hammers to make high quality rag paper.

▶ **STANDON**
The High Street c1965
S377012

In many a village, the loss of its transport system and main employer in the course of a couple of years would have sounded its death knell; but for Standon the situation could not have been more different. The corn mill burned down in 1961, and then in 1964 Dr Beeching swung his axe and the pretty railway line from Buntingford to Ware was closed. All was set for Standon to slip into a decline. However, the village thrives today. It rarely looks back to the past and to the time when, for example, Daniel Clerk the grave digger kept a large basket of human bones in his kitchen, claiming that he knew whose remains each was. Maybe some things are best forgotten!

◀ **STANDON**
The High Street c1955
S377005

The parish church of St Mary at Standon has a three-stage detached tower - one of the few in England. It is said to have been built by the Knights Hospitallers as a 'processional' church - again, one of only three in England. The Windmill pub stands out as the white building in the centre left of the view. The building in front of the church was the vicarage; it replaced the original, which stood in Burr's meadow behind the concrete posts and fencing on the left of the picture. The old vicarage and its two adjacent properties are known locally as the 'Three Bears.' None of the other buildings owns up to being Goldilocks!

▼ **BRAUGHING,** *The River Rib at Gatesbury c1960* B411014

Gatesbury lies to the east of the B1368 close to the junction for Puckeridge. Although originally part of the parish of Westmill, Gatesbury is now firmly within the parish of Braughing; it is named after the Gatesbury family, who held the manor from the late 1100s up to the 1400s, when it was passed to the FitzHerberts. But the history of Gatesbury goes back further, for Braughing was a Roman industrial centre for the manufacture of pottery. Examples can be found all over Roman Britain. When the River Rib is in full flood, bricks, tiles and other more interesting artefacts from the Roman settlement are washed from its banks and deposited in the slow-moving, gravelly meanders.

▶ **BRAUGHING,** *The Maltings and St Mary's Church c1960* B411016

The black-faced Maltings look out across the peaceful River Rib. Upstream, a few hundred yards before the river reaches the churchyard, the ford over the river is jealously guarded by the village ducks, geese and swans, who challenge pedestrians and motorists; usually, motorists take precedence, but not here at Braughing. St Mary's was the site of the

premature funeral of Matthew Wall. When he 'died' in 1574, one of the bearers slipped on the wet leaves, dropped his coffin and broke the lid. Out sprang Matthew, not dead but sleeping. He lived to a ripe old age, and when he finally died he left a legacy, still observed today, to pay for the path to be swept clear of leaves on the anniversary of his first funeral.

◀ WESTMILL
The Village Green
c1960 W295004

This village of great beauty is said to be the most photographed in Hertfordshire. The post office and shop now also serve as a successful tea shop, and display examples of the work of local artists and craftsmen. Peeping behind the pump cover is the unique timber-framed Village Hall - a monument to the Arts and Crafts movement. Westmill stood near the northern end of the now-closed Buntingford Branch Railway line, and was famous for its almost forgotten Folk Museum. It was the home of Nathaniel Salmon, one of the earliest Hertfordshire historians.

BUNTINGFORD
River Green
Bridge c1955
B245023

This bridge over the River Rib was built by Charles Gray in October 1852 at a cost of £95. In 1994, it was found to be unsafe and was totally rebuilt. The road over the bridge leads to Layston church via the elm-lined Causeway. Sad to tell, the avenue fell victim to Dutch elm disease.

▶ **BUNTINGFORD**
*High Street and
Market Hill c1955*
B245008

Buntingford was
founded in the 1100s
and served as a
market for the
surrounding villages
and communities,
particularly the
settlement at the
adjacent Layston. The
weekly cattle market,
revived in 1920, was
based on a royal
charter of 1542. The
tall building in the left
distance was
originally the Manse,
and became a shop in
the 1930s.

◀ **BUNTINGFORD**
*The Adam & Eve Public
House, London Road c1955*
B245009

The Adam & Eve was a
popular stopping place for
cyclists in the 1920s and
1930s. After its closure in the
1950s, the buildings were
taken down and it became
the site of a petrol station and
tyre-fitting business; but in
the late 1990s, this in turn was
demolished. The area is now
the site of a complex of
detached executive homes.
Peeping over the skyline is the
tower and spire of the Roman
Catholic church of St Richard.

▲ **BUNTINGFORD,** *Layston Church c1955* B245011

The present Layston church, the original parish church for Buntingford, was constructed on the site of an earlier building in the 13th century, and additions were built in the 15th century. The photograph shows the beginnings of the dereliction which has taken over the nave today. Only the tower and chancel, now used as a cemetery chapel, survive. As this book is published, considerable concern is being expressed with regard to the already over-full graveyard, and its future is being actively discussed.

◄**BARKWAY**
Main Street c1960 B281012

In 1700s and 1800s, Barkway lay on the main coach route from London to Cambridge. The Angel Inn (later the Wheatsheaf) served as the main staging post for travellers. In the early 1800s, it was owned by William Woolard, whose Newfoundland dog, Neptune, guarded the gate at the far end of the building. William Phelps, alias Brighton Bill, the pugilist, died here after his brutal encounter with Owen Swift in 1838. The white milestone (centre) is the last of a series measuring the route to Cambridge. The stones were erected in the early 1700s by Drs Mouse and Hare of Cambridge University.

▼ ROYSTON, *The Roundabout c1965* R63043

The roundabout is situated at the crossing of the Icknield Way (the A505) and the A10. Up to the southern border of Royston, the A10 follows the route of the Roman Ermine Street, but close to the market Ermine Street becomes the Old North Road (which was the A14 and is now the A1198) taking travellers to Godmanchester and Huntingdon, whilst the A10 branches to Cambridge. With the demise of the coach trade along the B1368 via Barkway, the A10 shown here was the main road from London to Cambridge. Although our picture is remarkably free of traffic, during holiday times cars, buses and lorries backed up for two or three miles in each direction, and the congestion was only relieved by the construction of the Royston northern by-pass in the late 1960s.

▶ ROYSTON
The Parish Church c1965 R63042

The church of St John the Baptist at Royston was originally part of the 13th-century priory. At the Dissolution, the nave was demolished and the western arch of the tower was filled in. The people of the town bought the remains of the original building, and it then became the parish church. Some of the original small lancet windows and the early south aisle timber roof are still visible. Close to the church and the Cross, an ancient glacial boulder cut with a slot to hold a market cross, lies the intriguing underground Royston Cave. The gloomy light reveals a myriad of medieval relief carvings depicting, some believe, Knights Templar symbols and mystic signs.

◄ASHWELL
The Chantry House c1955
A149002

The thatched roof and plastered walls of the Chantry House typify the construction of the houses and cottages in Ashwell. Even the barn (left, behind the delivery van) is thatched. More expensive later buildings were of brick with a tiled roof, although, of course, the earlier church is built of stone. There is a village story that one Friday evening around 1850, Georgianna Covington was on her way to choir practice when she noticed a figure coming towards her. As she entered the church, she turned and to her horror saw that the hooded apparition had no head. She staggered into the church and fell senseless on the floor of the chancel, causing fear and fright amongst the choir who were assembling there.

ASHWELL
Foresters Cottages, High Street c1955 A149006

The cottages were threatened with destruction shortly after this photograph was taken, but popular opinion prevailed and they were saved. The Hertfordshire Building Preservation Trust, in collaboration with Hertfordshire County Council, carried out a major restoration in the 1960s, and they now stand proudly as a memorial to what might have been lost. Almost opposite Foresters Cottages is the headquarters of the Veteran Car Club of Great Britain, and members' cars often visit the village. Spring afternoons provide a fine sight as some of these elderly 'ladies and gentlemen' parade through the streets and lanes.

ASHWELL
The Village Museum
c1960 A149042

Truly one of the finest small museums in Hertfordshire, Ashwell Village Museum was founded in November 1930 and is based on the collection of Albert Sheldrick and John Bray, made when they were schoolboys. Probably its most attractive artefact is the building itself, which was constructed in the early 16th century: the Town House was owned by Westminster Abbey and later by St John's College, Cambridge, and was used to collect rents and tithes. Later on it was used by one of the village tailors as a workshop, but it fell into disrepair; it was eventually saved, at a cost of £25, to become the museum.

73

▶ **ASHWELL,** *The Parish Church of St Mary the Virgin c1955* A149012

The spire of St Mary's dominates the village and the surrounding countryside. It has overlooked pleasure, tragedy and, it is said, the supernatural. When the Black Death raged through Europe, Ashwell was not spared, and a desperate villager scratched on the wall of the church: '1350 - miserable wild distracted the dregs of the people alone survive to witness and tell the tale'. This is the tale of the great storm which was believed to have blown away the last infectious air. Another graffito demonstrates the frustration of the stonemason - it reads: 'the corners are not set correctly - I spit on them'.

▼ **BALDOCK,** *White Horse Street c1960* B9040

The Rose & Crown (left) was 'a Family & Residential Hotel'; next door was the Greyhound. The missing sign above the glass canopy read 'Teas'. The striped blinds in the distance belong to Booths, ironmonger and draper. The last of the five hitching posts stills stands outside the Rose & Crown, a popular stopping place for cyclists and motorists. In October 1903, William and Ernest Hart, driving their 24hp Darracq, rested at the Rose & Crown, and reported, 'Had three punctures in 50 miles ... cracked differential case, noisy gears and all sorts of trouble. Glad to turn into this haven of rest'.

▶ BALDOCK
The Gates c1960
B9032

The gates were said to have come from the Leper Hospital at Clothall. Close to the John Wynne Almshouses, buses turned in front of the buildings and the open space was used for stalls on market day and for attractions when the fair came to the town. The Mayflower Gift Shop survives, but much else has changed.

BALDOCK
High Street c1955 B9014

A rare Lea Francis convertible is parked outside Randolph Antiques. Between the houses in the distance was the site of the Roman Catholic church dedicated to the Holy Trinity and St Augustine of Canterbury in 1926; it was never completed, and the remains were demolished in 1977. Next door to Randolph's stands the Cock pub, an old establishment and one of a portfolio of Baldock public houses owned by John Izzard Prior in 1823. The gardens in the foreground are at the corner of Mansfield Road close to the Lodge. The Lodge was originally the entrance to Elmwood House, located close to the site of the Kayser Bondor factory built c1919 for the Full-Fashioned Hosiery Company - this later became a large Tesco store.

NORTON

The Parish Church and the Village c1950 N196038

This quiet north Hertfordshire village offers teas in the garden - or something a little stronger at the Three Horseshoes (left). The pub had been the village school in 1873. In the background is the 12th-century parish church of St Nicholas, which has been superseded by the ultra-modern church of St George in the 'new' town of Letchworth. St Nicholas' is particularly proud of its peal of eight bells, which includes one cast in the 1500s and another, recast in 1946, in memory of the travelling evangelist, Gypsy Smith.

LETCHWORTH, *The Council Offices c1950* L39005

The Georgian-style council offices, now North Herts District Council's housing department, were built for the Urban District Council in 1935 to a design by Bennet & Bidwell, architects of many of the buildings in the town. In the background is the Broadway cinema at the junction of Gernon Road and Eastcheap. It opened on 26 August 1936, and the first film to be shown was 'Follow the Fleet' starring Fred Astaire and Ginger Rogers.

ICKLEFORD
*St Katharine's Parish Church
and the Lychgate c1960*
I36013

St Katharine was the patron saint of millers, saddlers, wheelwrights and teachers - all trades and professions which appropriately flourished in Ickleford. A tunnel leads from the church to the nearby Old George public house. It runs beneath the car park, but has now been blocked off. Built in the 12th century, St Katharine's was reconstructed in 1859 by gift of the Ryder family under the direction of Sir Giles Gilbert Scott. In the churchyard stands the grave of Henry Boswell, a gypsy king, who boasted that he lived through the reign of three Georges and that he knew every road in the land.

ICKLEFORD, *Thatched Cottage c1960* I36009

This charming timber framed cottage (with a relatively modern extension) is a typical product of the skill of local carpenters and builders. Arts and crafts have always been an important facet of this community. In the late 1800s, Walter Witter and his son, Carl, ran evening classes in tapestry and copper work. They began a local business, and in 1939 transferred the tapestry workshop to Cambridge, leaving the metalwork in the hands of local craftsmen, Olney and Newbury. A product of the tapestry workers, made for the Silver Jubilee of King George V, survived the disastrous fire at Windsor Castle in the late 1990s.

► **HITCHIN**
Bancroft c1955 H89015

When in the 1950s Reginald Hine, the great Hitchin historian, wrote of the town, 'It is lamentable what we have lost during the last 100 years', he was complaining of the desecration of the buildings and streets and the poor architecture of the environment that we see in this photograph. Things have changed again during the past fifty or so years. What would Hine have said about Hitchin in the 21st century?

► **HITCHIN**
The Market 1965 H89087

The jam-packed stalls of Hitchin market reflect the higgledy-piggledy dwellings that it replaced. The programme of urban clearance started in 1923 may have been prompted by comments like that of John Thompson, who spoke one hundred years previously of the 'very depressed and profligate inhabitants of Hollow Lane and Dead Street which, from generation to generation, was known for the filth and deprivation of its inhabitants'.

HITCHIN
Brand Street c1955
H89036

The smooth tarmaced
surface of Brand Street
contrasts with the rutted
and rough surface of the
1800s. Indeed, the story
is told that the road was
so bad that one of the
potholes was filled with a
fully harnessed dead
cart-horse. On the right,
the building on the far
side of the post office
(built 1903) is the
Methodist Wesleyan
chapel which was
opened on 24 July 1834.

HITCHIN
The Old Market Place
1965 H89057

A motor historian's delight, this view of the old Market Place shows it being used as a car park on market day. Apart from the ubiquitous Minis, Morris Minors and Ford 105E Anglias, we can see not one but two examples of the rare Austin Metropolitan, two Jaguar Mk IIs, a Vauxhall VX 4/90 and a Vauxhall PA Cresta. In the 1960s this was a prosperous town, and a far cry from the time when this was part of the 'vile slum' area of Hitchin.

▼ **BREACHWOOD GREEN**, *Lower Road c1965* B412025

Outside the row of terraced cottages at Breachwood Green near Hitchin stands a pristine Ford 100E model. In front of one of these houses stood the community's well. This was cemented over in the 1950s. It was 175 feet deep, and was notorious for breaking its rope and losing the bucket. This had to be fished out using a hooked heavy iron 'strudgel', which was lowered on a strong cable and scraped around the bottom until it caught on the handle of the bucket so that it could be brought to the surface.

▶ **KIMPTON**
The High Street c1960
K94002

Kimpton was one of the Hertfordshire villages that kept up the tradition of celebrating May Day. A May Queen would be crowned on the village green, and the children paraded through the village wearing colourful costumes. Later in the day they would weave intricate patterns with the ribbons as they danced round the maypole. But the children were not always so well behaved, for in 1518 it was reported that the service was often disturbed by babies 'laughing, crying and even singing in church'.

◄ **KIMPTON**
The White Horse
c1960 K94010

In 1837, the White Horse
was just a small beer
house. It was recorded
as 'a cottage and a
garden owned by
John Marshall of
Hitchin and occupied
by Sarah Buckle, widow'.
Nearby stood the Two
Brewers public house.
As trade at the White
Horse flourished, that
at the Two Brewers
declined, and it was
closed in 1915.

CODICOTE
The George and Dragon c1960
C320045

The George and Dragon is first mentioned as a tavern in the court book of St Albans Abbey in 1279. The half-timbered building dates from the 17th century. In 1967, 'Trencherman', writing for 'Hertfordshire 'Countryside magazine, reported that the bill for a three-course meal for two cost £3 2s 8d (£3.18), and that the main course of two(!)

rainbow trout cooked in butter with almonds was priced at 11s 6d (62p). The half-bottle of red wine cost 4s 6d (42p). But bear in mind that a meal there in 1650 would have cost about 6d (2p).

CODICOTE, *The Village c1955* C320024

The village lies along the old turnpike road about halfway between Hatfield and Hitchin. On the right, a road branches off to Wheathampstead. Codicote had a number of interesting charities. In one, the rent of five closes of land in Berden, Essex, was to pay for the apprenticeship of a young lad from the village. Another refers to a plot of land called 'The Labour in Vain'.

AYOT ST LAWRENCE, *The Old Church c1955* A99002

The remains of the old church lie to the west of the village. It was built in the 12th century with later additions and renovations, including the tower of around 1500. The church fell into disuse when the new church was built in 1799. When he built Ayot House, Sir Leonard Lyde found that the old church had blocked his view, and began to demolish it without permission from the bishop. He was forced to cease the desecration as soon as news reached the bishop, but the work had proceeded too far, and the ruins stand today as a reminder of his folly.

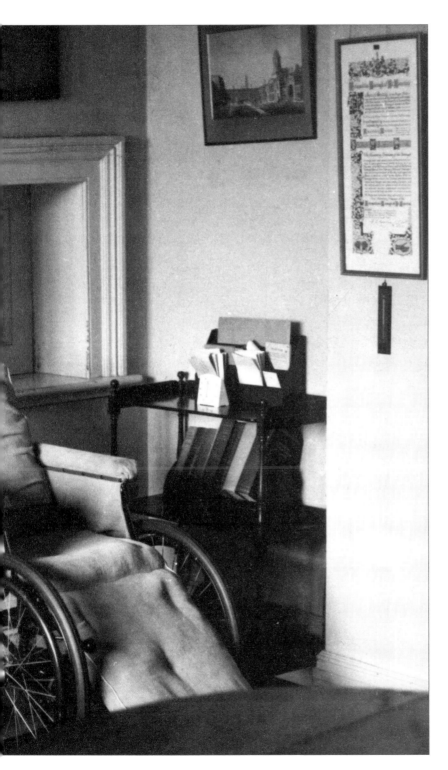

AYOT ST LAWRENCE
Shaw's Corner, The New Rectory c1955 A99011

The home of George Bernard Shaw has remained unchanged since his death: his hat still hangs in the hall, whilst his typewriter stands on his study desk where he wrote 'Pygmalion', 'Back to Methuselah' and 'Saint Joan'. It is said that he chose the village as his home when he noticed a tombstone in the churchyard which reads: 'Mary Ann South, born 1825, died 1895. Her time was short' - if 70 years was short, he was sure that this was the place for him. Indeed, GBS lived for 94 years, and died in the garden of the New Rectory after falling from a ladder whilst pruning his fruit trees. The house and its contents, including the photographs of prominent Socialist leaders (on the mantelpiece, left), were bequeathed to the National Trust; they, and the annual Midsummer Art Festival, attract many visitors every year.

▶ **AYOT ST LAWRENCE**
The Village c1950
A99010

The post office at Ayot was used by George Bernard Shaw in a rather lesser known play, 'A Village Wooing'. The postmistress, Miss Jisbella Lyth, was a personal friend, and considered it an honour to deal with his voluminous mail. The village had been owned by the fathers of the Cathedral of Westminster, but it was passed to the descendants of the Norman de Mandeville family in 1120.

◀ **WHEATHAMPSTEAD**
Brewhouse Hill c1960
W296045

Brewhouse Hill leads from Wheathampstead to the hamlet of Amwell (not to be confused with the village, south of Ware, of the same name.) The almost new Vauxhall Wyvern E model is parked nearly opposite Collins, the antique dealer, and adjacent to the rather modern houses behind the slag-block wall. The village was the home of the Cherry-Garrard family, one of whom was with Scott on his ill-fated expedition to the South Pole.

▲ **HARPENDEN,** *Rothampstead Agricultural Experimental Station c1960* H25019

Rothampstead, for 600 years in the hands of the Cressys, the Bardolphs and the Wittewronge-Lawes, lies close to the St Albans Road. Although the estate dates from only the 1300s, it is thought that the site may date back to the Roman period, for the remains of a Belgic shrine has been found in the grounds. The present building has a core which was built around 1600, but it has been enlarged and altered to its present size.

◀**HARPENDEN**
The Pond on the Common c1960
H25015

On the third Tuesday in September, the Harpenden Statty Fair (Statute Fair) was held on the common close to the pond and the adjacent Triangle. In the late 1800s, the fair was illuminated by gas, but after the turn of the century, the steam-driven generators lit the stalls with electricity. The steam engines drew their water from the ponds. Children and young adults enjoyed the roundabouts, the cake-walk, the swings, the coconut shies and the side shows. Another fair was held on Bank Holiday Monday, and one elderly lady remembered collecting discarded ginger beer bottles to exchange for the refund of one penny after the fair had closed down for the day.

HARPENDEN
The High Street c1960
H25061

The A6 road runs across the Common at Harpenden, under the 'Baa Lamb' trees and into the High Street. Nobody knows for certain why they are called the 'Baa Lamb Trees'; it has been suggested that this was where the local shepherd sat whilst tending his flock. The shops sit cheek by jowl on one side of the street, whilst the other is fringed with pollarded limes and chestnuts. In these days before the drink-drive laws, the owner of the Morris Minor van has popped into the White Lion (right) for quiet pint. How similar this is to the travellers who have used the road since before Roman times and would have sought rest and refreshment at Harpenden.

▶ **REDBOURN**
The Jolly Gardeners c1955
R87009

Considered to be the oldest house in the village, the Jolly Gardeners is now a private dwelling. In the distance on the right stands the parish church, which dates from Norman times. It boasts one of the finest carved rood screens in the county - it is mentioned in the church records of 1479.

◀ **REDBOURN**
The Aubreys c1955 R87020

On the level ground to the south-west of the town stands the almost ploughed-out remains of an ancient double-ditched camp called The Aubreys. Close by stood a house called The Aubreys, later the Aubrey Park Hotel, a fine part mock-Tudor building graced, in this view, by an elegant Humber Pullman limousine.
It was originally Foster's Farm, and was owned by the Dunn family, the London hat makers. After its conversion, The Aubreys was used for a short time as a holiday centre for children from Bethnal Green.

REDBOURN
The Memorial and the Village c1955 R87007

On 24 June 1827, William Cobbett wrote in his 'Rural Rides': 'Set out at four this morning for Redbourn. The trees ... are very fine: oak, ashes and beeches; some of the finest of each sort. The hedges are full with shepherd's rose, honeysuckles and all sorts of flowers, with the most beautiful of all flower gardens and shrubberies on your one hand and corn on the other. What can equal these fields in Hertfordshire?' Maybe our view lacks the shrubberies, flowers and corn, but little else would have changed since Cobbett's time.

▶ **REDBOURN**
The High Street c1955
R87001

It was along this street that the men of the town swarmed in 1381 towards St Albans. They demanded and received a charter protecting their right of pasture, fisheries and so on. After the death of Wat Tyler, the Peasants' Revolt collapsed, and many of these concessions, but not all, were revoked. In 'Hertfordshire Countryside' for January 1970, W G S Crook writes: 'I cannot recollect ever finding Redbourn High Street deserted.' Frith's photographer would have begged to differ.

▶ **REDBOURN**
The High Street c1965
R87036

It is a few years after No R87001 (above), and the High Street is still almost deserted - just a couple of cars but no pedestrians, despite the new-fangled zebra crossing. As every school child knows, the Romans built long straight roads; Redbourn High Street is no exception, for it forms part of the Roman Watling Street. It was along this road that the body of King Edward I's wife, Eleanor, was brought on its journey from Lincoln to London. In 1554,

the sick and feeble Princess Elizabeth (later Queen Elizabeth I) was dragged from her bed at Ashridge to be brought to the Tower of London. She was so weak that her first overnight stop was at Redbourn. A hundred and seventy years ago, a Dr Stephens lived in the High Street. His invention of blue-black ink made him world famous.

▲ **ST ALBANS,** *The Abbey from Verulamium Park c1955* S2039

In 739, the Mercian king Offa founded a Benedictine house for men and women, which he endowed with huge tracts of Hertfordshire countryside together with their rents and tithes. The building of the present abbey began in 1077 when Paul de Caen, a Norman abbot, set about erecting the second longest church in Britain. Much of the original structure was built using rubble from the remains of the Roman town of Verulamium, which stood close to the present Verulamium Park.

◄ **HATFIELD**
St Etheldreda's Church c1950
H254057

In 'Pride and Prejudice' Jane Austen calls Hatfield 'a busy little street that leads to my Lord Salisbury's house'. Opposite the old Salisbury Arms public house in Fore Street stands St Etheldreda's church. It dates from the 13th century and contains the Salisbury Chapel, built in 1618 to hold the tomb of Robert Cecil, first earl of Salisbury, at a cost of £460. Clearly, this was a town dominated by the Salisbury family and their home at Hatfield House. However, when Charles Dickens visited the house, he was more impressed by the earl's huge gooseberries than his huge house! But later, during his visit in 1835 as a young cub newspaper reporter, he witnessed the burning of the west wing when the first marchioness was burnt to death after knocking over a lighted candle.

▶ **WELWYN GARDEN CITY**
Welwyn Stores c1955 W294020

The first Welwyn Stores was founded in 1921 at Guessens road, but it closed in July 1939 when the new, larger stores was opened in the centre of the new town. Welwyn Stores had branches in many towns in Hertfordshire, and formed an important part of the Garden City Company. In 1947, Welwyn Stores contributed £1,560,000 to the company's gross income.

◄**WELWYN GARDEN CITY**
The Memorial and
Hollybush Lane c1955
W294034

Hollybush Lane lies in
the southern part of the
Garden City, and its tree-lined
footpath and grassy
triangular area typify
Ebenezer Howard's vision of a
ordered village atmosphere.
He imagined a community
living within a country town
landscape benefiting from
modern amenities and
facilities. Like its near
neighbour at Letchworth,
Welwyn Garden City
successfully achieves all his
requirements.

WELWYN GARDEN CITY
*The Fountain, Parkway
c1955* W294010

Today, we feel that when
Louis de Soissions designed
the layout of the Garden
City, he underestimated the
impact of the motor car.
However, it would appear
from this photograph that
he was correct in his
predictions. Not a car or van
spoils the gossiping ladies'
view of the Parkway and the
fountain. Ten years later it
would be a different story,
and special parking
provisions would have to be
made to accommodate the
huge amount of road traffic.

▼ DIGSWELL, *The Welwyn Viaduct c1960* D223005

The 1560ft-long Welwyn viaduct at Digswell carries the London to Peterborough railway 100ft above the River Mimram a mile or so north of Welwyn Garden City. Opened on Monday 6 August 1850, the 40 semi-circular arches are built from sixteen million locally made bricks capped with Hexham stone blocks; the cost was £80,000. It was the third largest viaduct in Great Britain - only Stockport and Congleton were larger. A year after its opening, on 28 August 1851, Queen Victoria's Royal Train crossed the viaduct as it took the royal family to Balmoral Castle.

▶ DIGSWELL
*The Post Office
c1960* D223012

The post office and shop survived until about 1995, when the premises were taken over by Weddinghouse, a business selling and hiring wedding dresses and costumes. The post box still stands in the garden of the shop at the corner of Station Road and Woodside Road, but the telephone box, peeping into the left of the photograph, has disappeared.

◄ **DIGSWELL**
The Cowper Arms
c1960 D223001

The Cowper Arms lies at the corner of Colyer Close and Station Road. In the 1850s, when a terrible accident occurred in the nearby railway tunnel, some of the bodies were brought here in preparation for the inquest. Today, the house has changed little, although the black barn has been demolished. Also, with the conversion of the railway from steam to electricity, the overhead wiring is strung along the skyline.

WATTON AT STONE
The Parish Church of St Andrew and St Mary c1960 W292019

There has been a church at Watton at Stone since the 13th century. It was originally dedicated to St Mary, but St Andrew seems to have been added in the early 19th century. During the Civil War, the Commonwealth soldiers used the church as a prison for their Royalist captives. Although much of the church is original 16th-century - the north chapel was built in 1570 - extensions and restorations were carried out in 1851 at a cost of £7,000. The tower is said to be haunted by a grey lady who threw herself from the top when she was spurned in love. It is an interesting fact that the present bells are not original: they were brought to Watton from a church in north London in 1978. In 1960, at nearby Stoney Hill, bricks were still being made by hand. Four brick makers were moulding and firing about 3,200 bricks per day. Every ten days, the kilns were fired in the outlying fields, and there appeared to be a guaranteed and continuing market for their product.

▶ DATCHWORTH
The Green and the Whipping Post c1965
D122003

Behind the Best Kept Village sign (centre) stands Datchworth's whipping post. It is said that it was last used in 1665 when 'two vagabonds were publicly flogged here'. Up to two hundred years ago, the whipping of vagrants was a common practice; it seems that Datchworth was rather more understanding than most other villages and ceased the practice around the time of the Plague of London. A beautiful and ornate new village sign, commemorating the turn of the millennium, has replaced the Best Kept Village sign; as well, of course, as a mention of the whipping post, this shows the village at work and at play. The plaque says that it was given 'To the village, for the village, from the village'.

◄ DATCHWORTH
The Post Office and the Plough c1965 D122006

The 17th-century post office stands at the corner of Bramfield Road and Mardlebury Road. It and the Plough beyond have today changed little since this photograph was taken. The telephone box is still in the same position, although a new brick-based post box has been installed, and goods for sale have now spilled out onto the pavement. Now, there is a low fence around of the Plough, which sells the finest Greene King beers. A parish notice board has been erected in the pillared garden of the next door cottage.

DATCHWORTH
The Tilbury c1965
D122018

The pub was originally called the Tilbury Fort. The name and licence were moved from a public house standing on the corner of the churchyard and owned by the parish. The rent was paid to the Overseer for the relief of the poor. In 1838 the house was bought from the parish by William and Joseph Lucas, the Hitchin brewers, who transferred the sign and licence to the already existing Three Horsehoes.

KNEBWORTH
London Road c1965
K43030

Not to be confused with
Old Knebworth (which one
recent historian described
as 'a village still faintly
feudal in character'), the
village of Knebworth is a
busy commercial centre
supplying the needs of the
surrounding communities.
All the needs of a
developing small town are
in evidence - the Bedford
lorry loaded with builders
materials, Charles Love &
Son's ironmongery and
radio/TV engineer's (right),
Lisles petrol station (near
right), and further down the
road, car sales showrooms
as well as the usual high
street shops and stores.
Within a few years,
London Road would
become a busy and
congested thoroughfare for
travellers from the new
town at Stevenage (a few
miles to the north) and the
outskirts of London.

BENNINGTON
St Peter's Church c1960 B406022

It is recorded that the site of the present St Peter's Church was used as a place of worship as early as the 9th century at the time of King Bertulph of Mercia. After the Norman Conquest, the manor was held by Peter de Valoignes, and it was from him that the church took its dedication. The building has been restored on number of occasions, and when the tower was renovated in the early part of the last century, some of the stone heads were re-carved to represent the workmen. One particular head resembles Josef Stalin wearing his renowned cap - however, in fact it represents David Warner, the sexton. It is believed that he negotiated a deal with the mason. 'Give me a price of a mug of ale', the mason is said to have told him, 'and I'll put your mug on the tower!'

STEVENAGE, *The Bowling Green c1950* S191008

Looking across the bowling green, we can see the Publix Cinema. It is showing 'Jungle Jim' starring Johnny Weissmuller, ex-Tarzan, and features the yet-to-be-famous Superman actor, George Reeves. 'Jungle Jim' was one of the worst of the 'Jungle' film genre - one reviewer wrote that 'Jungle Jim' had 'no particular personality or background'. The Publix struggled on for a few more years, but it finally succumbed and closed when the Astoria opened in the new town. The war memorial was dedicated in 1921. Shortly afterwards, the open bowling green was fenced off.

STEVENAGE
The Cromwell Hotel c1955
S191043

The building behind the Hillman Minx was originally the home of the Courbold-Ellis family. It is thought to have started life as a farmhouse, and was possibly owned by John Thurloe, Oliver Cromwell's Secretary of State. The Courbold-Ellises owned it until the 1930s, when it became a hotel. The Cromwell, with its illuminated fish pond in the forecourt, was a popular stopping place for travellers; among its famous regulars was Sir Henry Wood, the musical conductor and founder of the Albert Hall Promenade concerts.

STEVENAGE, *Haydene c1955* S191073

Stevenage was the first of a series of post-Second World War new towns ringing London. Initially, Knebworth had been suggested, but it was felt that railway provision was better at Stevenage. It was envisaged that the population of Stevenage would increase from 7,000 to 60,000 in the following twenty years, and indeed 67.000 people lived in the town in 1971.

WALKERN
Church End c1960
W289006

Walkern was the home of Joan Wenham, one of the last witches to be prosecuted in England. There are many accounts of the case, but one interesting version says that it hinged on her ability to fly. The judge dismissed the charge of witchcraft, and challenged anybody to prove that flying was illegal. Eventually, Joan went to live at Gilston and died at Hertingfordbury in 1730.

WALKERN, *The High Street c1960* W289003

Although in 1960 Walkern was a peaceful village, its history included many scenes of violence. During the Civil War, the rector, John Gorsuch, was smothered in a haystack by two of Cromwell's supporters. Later on, in 1728, when returning from the market at Hertford, Thomas Adams was violently murdered in the High Street.

INDEX

Frith Book Co Titles

www.francisfrith.co.uk

The Frith Book Company publishes over 100 new titles each year. A selection of those currentl available is listed below. For latest catalogue please contact Frith Book Co.
Town Books 96 pages, approximately 100 photos. **County and Themed Books** 128 pages, approximately 150 photos (unless specified). All titles hardback with laminated case and jacke except those indicated pb (paperback)

Amersham, Chesham & Rickmansworth (pb)	1-85937-340-2	£9.99	Devon (pb)	1-85937-297-x	£9.9
Andover (pb)	1-85937-292-9	£9.99	Devon Churches (pb)	1-85937-250-3	£9.9
Aylesbury (pb)	1-85937-227-9	£9.99	Dorchester (pb)	1-85937-307-0	£9.9
Barnstaple (pb)	1-85937-300-3	£9.99	Dorset (pb)	1-85937-269-4	£9.9
Basildon Living Memories (pb)	1-85937-515-4	£9.99	Dorset Coast (pb)	1-85937-299-6	£9.9
Bath (pb)	1-85937-419-0	£9.99	Dorset Living Memories (pb)	1-85937-584-7	£9.9
Bedford (pb)	1-85937-205-8	£9.99	Down the Severn (pb)	1-85937-560-x	£9.9
Bedfordshire Living Memories	1-85937-513-8	£14.99	Down The Thames (pb)	1-85937-278-3	£9.9
Belfast (pb)	1-85937-303-8	£9.99	Down the Trent	1-85937-311-9	£14.9
Berkshire (pb)	1-85937-191-4	£9.99	East Anglia (pb)	1-85937-265-1	£9.9
Berkshire Churches	1-85937-170-1	£17.99	East Grinstead (pb)	1-85937-138-8	£9.9
Berkshire Living Memories	1-85937-332-1	£14.99	East London	1-85937-080-2	£14.9
Black Country	1-85937-497-2	£12.99	East Sussex (pb)	1-85937-606-1	£9.9
Blackpool (pb)	1-85937-393-3	£9.99	Eastbourne (pb)	1-85937-399-2	£9.9
Bognor Regis (pb)	1-85937-431-x	£9.99	Edinburgh (pb)	1-85937-193-0	£8.9
Bournemouth (pb)	1-85937-545-6	£9.99	England In The 1880s	1-85937-331-3	£17.9
Bradford (pb)	1-85937-204-x	£9.99	Essex - Second Selection	1-85937-456-5	£14.9
Bridgend (pb)	1-85937-386-0	£7.99	Essex (pb)	1-85937-270-8	£9.9
Bridgwater (pb)	1-85937-305-4	£9.99	Essex Coast	1-85937-342-9	£14.9
Bridport (pb)	1-85937-327-5	£9.99	Essex Living Memories	1-85937-490-5	£14.9
Brighton (pb)	1-85937-192-2	£8.99	Exeter	1-85937-539-1	£9.9
Bristol (pb)	1-85937-264-3	£9.99	Exmoor (pb)	1-85937-608-8	£9.9
British Life A Century Ago (pb)	1-85937-213-9	£9.99	Falmouth (pb)	1-85937-594-4	£9.9
Buckinghamshire (pb)	1-85937-200-7	£9.99	Folkestone (pb)	1-85937-124-8	£9.9
Camberley (pb)	1-85937-222-8	£9.99	Frome (pb)	1-85937-317-8	£9.9
Cambridge (pb)	1-85937-422-0	£9.99	Glamorgan	1-85937-488-3	£14.9
Cambridgeshire (pb)	1-85937-420-4	£9.99	Glasgow (pb)	1-85937-190-6	£9.9
Cambridgeshire Villages	1-85937-523-5	£14.99	Glastonbury (pb)	1-85937-338-0	£7.9
Canals And Waterways (pb)	1-85937-291-0	£9.99	Gloucester (pb)	1-85937-232-5	£9.9
Canterbury Cathedral (pb)	1-85937-179-5	£9.99	Gloucestershire (pb)	1-85937-561-8	£9.9
Cardiff (pb)	1-85937-093-4	£9.99	Great Yarmouth (pb)	1-85937-426-3	£9.9
Carmarthenshire (pb)	1-85937-604-5	£9.99	Greater Manchester (pb)	1-85937-266-x	£9.9
Chelmsford (pb)	1-85937-310-0	£9.99	Guildford (pb)	1-85937-410-7	£9.9
Cheltenham (pb)	1-85937-095-0	£9.99	Hampshire (pb)	1-85937-279-1	£9.9
Cheshire (pb)	1-85937-271-6	£9.99	Harrogate (pb)	1-85937-423-9	£9.9
Chester (pb)	1-85937-382 8	£9.99	Hastings and Bexhill (pb)	1-85937-131-0	£9.9
Chesterfield (pb)	1-85937-378-x	£9.99	Heart of Lancashire (pb)	1-85937-197-3	£9.9
Chichester (pb)	1-85937-228-7	£9.99	Helston (pb)	1-85937-214-7	£9.9
Churches of East Cornwall (pb)	1-85937-249-x	£9.99	Hereford (pb)	1-85937-175-2	£9.9
Churches of Hampshire (pb)	1-85937-207-4	£9.99	Herefordshire (pb)	1-85937-567-7	£9.9
Cinque Ports & Two Ancient Towns	1-85937-492-1	£14.99	Herefordshire Living Memories	1-85937-514-6	£14.9
Colchester (pb)	1-85937-188-4	£8.99	Hertfordshire (pb)	1-85937-247-3	£9.9
Cornwall (pb)	1-85937-229-5	£9.99	Horsham (pb)	1-85937-432-8	£9.9
Cornwall Living Memories	1-85937-248-1	£14.99	Humberside (pb)	1-85937-605-3	£9.9
Cotswolds (pb)	1-85937-230-9	£9.99	Hythe, Romney Marsh, Ashford (pb)	1-85937-256-2	£9.9
Cotswolds Living Memories	1-85937-255-4	£14.99	Ipswich (pb)	1-85937-424-7	£9.9
County Durham (pb)	1-85937-398-4	£9.99	Isle of Man (pb)	1-85937-268-6	£9.9
Croydon Living Memories (pb)	1-85937-162-0	£9.99	Isle of Wight (pb)	1-85937-429-8	£9.9
Cumbria (pb)	1-85937-621-5	£9.99	Isle of Wight Living Memories	1-85937-304-6	£14.9
Derby (pb)	1-85937-367-4	£9.99	Kent (pb)	1-85937-189-2	£9.9
Derbyshire (pb)	1-85937-196-5	£9.99	Kent Living Memories(pb)	1-85937-401-8	£9.9
Derbyshire Living Memories	1-85937-330-5	£14.99	Kings Lynn (pb)	1-85937-334-8	£9.9

Available from your local bookshop or from the publisher

Frith Book Co Titles (continued)

Title	ISBN	Price	Title	ISBN	Price
e District (pb)	1-85937-275-9	£9.99	Sherborne (pb)	1-85937-301-1	£9.99
ncashire Living Memories	1-85937-335-6	£14.99	Shrewsbury (pb)	1-85937-325-9	£9.99
ncaster, Morecambe, Heysham (pb)	1-85937-233-3	£9.99	Shropshire (pb)	1-85937-326-7	£9.99
eds (pb)	1-85937-202-3	£9.99	Shropshire Living Memories	1-85937-643-6	£14.99
cester (pb)	1-85937-381-x		Somerset	1-85937-153-1	£14.99
cestershire & Rutland Living Memories	1-85937-500-6	£12.99	South Devon Coast	1-85937-107-8	£14.99
cestershire (pb)	1-85937-185-x	£9.99	South Devon Living Memories (pb)	1-85937-609-6	£9.99
hthouses	1-85937-257-0	£9.99	South East London (pb)	1-85937-263-5	£9.99
coln (pb)	1-85937-380-1	£9.99	South Somerset	1-85937-318-6	£14.99
colnshire (pb)	1-85937-433-6	£9.99	South Wales	1-85937-519-7	£14.99
erpool and Merseyside (pb)	1-85937-234-1	£9.99	Southampton (pb)	1-85937-427-1	£9.99
ndon (pb)	1-85937-183-3	£9.99	Southend (pb)	1-85937-313-5	£9.99
ndon Living Memories	1-85937-454-9	£14.99	Southport (pb)	1-85937-425-5	£9.99
dlow (pb)	1-85937-176-0	£9.99	St Albans (pb)	1-85937-341-0	£9.99
ton (pb)	1-85937-235-x	£9.99	St Ives (pb)	1-85937-415-8	£9.99
idenhead (pb)	1-85937-339-9	£9.99	Stafford Living Memories (pb)	1-85937-503-0	£9.99
idstone (pb)	1-85937-391-7	£9.99	Staffordshire (pb)	1-85937-308-9	£9.99
anchester (pb)	1-85937-198-1	£9.99	Stourbridge (pb)	1-85937-530-8	£9.99
rlborough (pb)	1-85937-336-4	£9.99	Stratford upon Avon (pb)	1-85937-388-7	£9.99
ddlesex	1-85937-158-2	£14.99	Suffolk (pb)	1-85937-221-x	£9.99
onmouthshire	1-85937-532-4	£14.99	Suffolk Coast (pb)	1-85937-610-x	£9.99
w Forest (pb)	1-85937-390-9	£9.99	Surrey (pb)	1-85937-240-6	£9.99
wark (pb)	1-85937-366-6	£9.99	Surrey Living Memories	1-85937-328-3	£14.99
wport, Wales (pb)	1-85937-258-9	£9.99	Sussex (pb)	1-85937-184-1	£9.99
wquay (pb)	1-85937-421-2	£9.99	Sutton (pb)	1-85937-337-2	£9.99
rfolk (pb)	1-85937-195-7	£9.99	Swansea (pb)	1-85937-167-1	£9.99
rfolk Broads	1-85937-486-7	£14.99	Taunton (pb)	1-85937-314-3	£9.99
rfolk Living Memories (pb)	1-85937-402-6	£9.99	Tees Valley & Cleveland (pb)	1-85937-623-1	£9.99
rth Buckinghamshire	1-85937-626-6	£14.99	Teignmouth (pb)	1-85937-370-4	£7.99
rth Devon Living Memories	1-85937-261-9	£14.99	Thanet (pb)	1-85937-116-7	£9.99
rth Hertfordshire	1-85937-547-2	£14.99	Tiverton (pb)	1-85937-178-7	£9.99
rth London (pb)	1-85937-403-4	£9.99	Torbay (pb)	1-85937-597-9	£9.99
rth Somerset	1-85937-302-x	£14.99	Truro (pb)	1-85937-598-7	£9.99
rth Wales (pb)	1-85937-298-8	£9.99	Victorian & Edwardian Dorset	1-85937-254-6	£14.99
rth Yorkshire (pb)	1-85937-236-8	£9.99	Victorian & Edwardian Kent (pb)	1-85937-624-X	£9.99
rthamptonshire Living Memories	1-85937-529-4	£14.99	Victorian & Edwardian Maritime Album (pb)	1-85937-622-3	£9.99
rthamptonshire	1-85937-150-7	£14.99	Victorian and Edwardian Sussex (pb)	1-85937-625-8	£9.99
rthumberland Tyne & Wear (pb)	1-85937-281-3	£9.99	Villages of Devon (pb)	1-85937-293-7	£9.99
rthumberland	1-85937-522-7	£14.99	Villages of Kent (pb)	1-85937-294-5	£9.99
rwich (pb)	1-85937-194-9	£8.99	Villages of Sussex (pb)	1-85937-295-3	£9.99
ttingham (pb)	1-85937-324-0	£9.99	Warrington (pb)	1-85937-507-3	£9.99
ttinghamshire (pb)	1-85937-187-6	£9.99	Warwick (pb)	1-85937-518-9	£9.99
ford (pb)	1-85937-411-5	£9.99	Warwickshire (pb)	1-85937-203-1	£9.99
fordshire (pb)	1-85937-430-1	£9.99	Welsh Castles (pb)	1-85937-322-4	£9.99
fordshire Living Memories	1-85937-525-1	£14.99	West Midlands (pb)	1-85937-289-9	£9.99
gnton (pb)	1-85937-374-7	£7.99	West Sussex (pb)	1-85937-607-x	£9.99
ak District (pb)	1-85937-280-5	£9.99	West Yorkshire (pb)	1-85937-201-5	£9.99
mbrokeshire	1-85937-262-7	£14.99	Weston Super Mare (pb)	1-85937-306-2	£9.99
nzance (pb)	1-85937-595-2	£9.99	Weymouth (pb)	1-85937-209-0	£9.99
terborough (pb)	1-85937-219-8	£9.99	Wiltshire (pb)	1-85937-277-5	£9.99
turesque Harbours	1-85937-208-2	£14.99	Wiltshire Churches (pb)	1-85937-171-x	£9.99
rs	1-85937-237-6	£17.99	Wiltshire Living Memories (pb)	1-85937-396-8	£9.99
mouth (pb)	1-85937-389-5	£9.99	Winchester (pb)	1-85937-428-x	£9.99
ole & Sandbanks (pb)	1-85937-251-1	£9.99	Windsor (pb)	1-85937-333-x	£9.99
eston (pb)	1-85937-212-0	£9.99	Wokingham & Bracknell (pb)	1-85937-329-1	£9.99
ading (pb)	1-85937-238-4	£9.99	Woodbridge (pb)	1-85937-498-0	£9.99
dhill to Reigate (pb)	1-85937-596-0	£9.99	Worcester (pb)	1-85937-165-5	£9.99
gwood (pb)	1-85937-384-4	£7.99	Worcestershire Living Memories	1-85937-489-1	£14.99
mford (pb)	1-85937-319-4	£9.99	Worcestershire	1-85937-152-3	£14.99
yal Tunbridge Wells (pb)	1-85937-504-9	£9.99	York (pb)	1-85937-199-x	£9.99
isbury (pb)	1-85937-239-2	£9.99	Yorkshire (pb)	1-85937-186-8	£9.99
arborough (pb)	1-85937-379-8	£9.99	Yorkshire Coastal Memories	1-85937-506-5	£14.99
venoaks and Tonbridge (pb)	1-85937-392-5	£9.99	Yorkshire Dales	1-85937-502-2	£14.99
effield & South Yorks (pb)	1-85937-267-8	£9.99	Yorkshire Living Memories (pb)	1-85937-397-6	£9.99

See Frith books on the internet at www.francisfrith.co.uk

FRITH PRODUCTS & SERVICES

Francis Frith would doubtless be pleased to know that the pioneering publishing venture he started in 1860 still continues today. Over a hundred and forty years later, The Francis Frith Collection continues in the same innovative tradition and is now one of the foremost publishers of vintage photographs in the world. Some of the current activities include:

Interior Decoration

Today Frith's photographs can be seen framed and as giant wall murals in thousands of pubs, restaurants, hotels, banks, retail stores and other public buildings throughout the country. In every case they enhance the unique local atmosphere of the places they depict and provide reminders of gentler days in an increasingly busy and frenetic world.

Product Promotions

Frith products are used by many major companies to promote the sales of their own products or to reinforce their own history and heritage. Frith promotions have been used by Hovis bread, Courage beers, Scots Porage Oats, Colman's mustard, Cadbury's foods, Mellow Birds coffee, Dunhill pipe tobacco, Guinness, and Bulmer's Cider.

Genealogy and Family History

As the interest in family history and roots grows world-wide, more and more people are turning to Frith's photographs of Great Britain for images of the towns, villages and streets where their ancestors lived; and, of course, photographs of the churches and chapels where their ancestors were christened, married and buried are an essential part of every genealogy tree and family album.

Frith Products

All Frith photographs are available Framed or just as Mounted Prints and Posters (size 23 x 16 inches). These may be ordered from the address below. From time to time other products - Address Books, Calendars, Table Mats, etc - are available.

The Internet

Already fifty thousand Frith photographs can be viewed and purchased on the internet through the Frith websites and a myriad of partner sites.

For more detailed information on Frith companies and products, look at these sites:

www.francisfrith.co.uk
www.francisfrith.com
(for North American visitors)

See the complete list of Frith Books at:

www.francisfrith.co.uk

This web site is regularly updated with the latest list of publications from the Frith Book Company. If you wish to buy books relating to another part of the country that your local bookshop does not stock, you may purchase on-line.

For further information, trade, or author enquiries please contact us at the address below:
The Francis Frith Collection, Frith's Barn, Teffont, Salisbury, Wiltshire, England SP3 5QP.
Tel: +44 (0)1722 716 376 Fax: +44 (0)1722 716 881 Email: sales@francisfrith.co.uk

See Frith books on the internet at www.francisfrith.co.uk